Overcome or Succumb

Controlling Anxiety, Fear and Panic to Conquer Life

You Will Turn the Tide

By The Irish Big Wave Surfer and Ocean Adventurer

Al Mennie

D1206427

Disclaimer

I have tried to recreate events, locales and conversations from my memories of them. In order to maintain their anonymity in some instances I have changed the names of individuals and places, I may have changed some identifying characteristics and details such as physical properties, occupations and places of residence.

Although the author and publisher have made every effort to ensure that the information in this book were correct at press time, the author and publisher do not assume and hereby disclaim any liability, to any party for any loss, damage or disruption caused by errors or omissions, whether such omissions result from negligence, accident or any other cause.

This book is not intended as a substitute for the medical advice of physicians, doctors or similarly qualified individuals or bodies. The reader should regularly consult a physician or doctor in matters relating to his/her health, and in particular with respect to any symptoms which may require diagnosis or medical attention.

The information in this book is meant to supplement, not replace, proper sport specific training, practice, tuition and coaching. Like any sport or activity involving speed, equipment, balance or environmental factors, big wave surfing and many other activities, pastimes and pursuits mentioned in this book pose some inherent risk. The authors and publisher advise readers to take full responsibility for their safety and know their limits. Before practising skills described in this book, be sure that your equipment is well maintained and do not take risks beyond your level of experience, aptitude, training and comfort level.

This book is not intended as advice of any sort and is not to be used in that way. This book is intended as reference only and is not a how-to guide.

To everyone swimming for the surface

and those swept away

To their brave rescuers

To the lost

Al Mennie

Never give up

You will turn the tide

Stand your ground

Wield your sword

Carry your fallen

Charge on

Al Mennie

Sara & Blyton

Al Mennie

OVERCOME OR SUCCUMB

Chapters

1

LET'S GO

Let me be clear right from the very start. I am a big wave surfer; I'm an adventurer. I am obsessed with the ocean; I am possessed by the ocean, and I have salt water running through my bloodline for generations before me. I am extremely comfortable where lots of people may be extremely uncomfortable. This lifestyle has taught and educated me in various ways how to handle myself among elements over which I have no control. I thrive on the mission, live for the unknown, and I live and breathe the ocean. I love nothing more than going out to sea in pursuit of huge waves and all that comes with it, the adrenaline, the ups, the downs, the terror, the excitement, the challenges, and the sense of achievement. What I am not is a university graduate in the diagnosis of, management of, handling of, prescribed treatment of Anxiety, Fear, Panic, or mental health. However, I believe that the knowledge I have gained through my experience of pushing through boundaries of fear and anxiety in various ways whilst pursuing huge waves far out at sea in the North Atlantic means I have something of real substance to offer everyone that feels their life is being constrained by feelings of fear, anxiety, or panic.

In my experience, fear and anxiety make the world feel like it is closing in around me, and I either choose to succumb to the overwhelming feelings or choose to overcome them and at times act subconsciously. At times, fear and anxiety are acceptable in my mind to a certain level, and in this book, I explain why. Panic, on the other hand, is not acceptable. Panic for me is complete loss of control, and it puts me at the mercy of the elements, the environment.

What is scary to one person is potentially not to someone else, but the key here is, it isn't that I'm not scared in what I do; in fact, it's that I am scared, but I go anyway because I believe in myself and my ability and in that of those around me. That approach leads to many great opportunities in life.

I'm not the guy who says he isn't scared. I do not have it all worked out, so please don't think that because I am writing a book on this that I am void of fear and anxiety. I have felt fear at various levels and in various ways, but I think I am relatively unique in that I have experienced it a lot for most of my life and dealing with it is normal to me. To surf big waves, I deal with the obvious fear of drowning, the fear of a life-changing injury to my body or to my brain from lack of oxygen, not getting back ashore from a location far out at sea, and about a million other intricate little details that can have a huge impact. The most important thing I must never do no matter how bad things get is panic. I am pursuing monstrous waves, waves the size of houses and beyond in the frigid North Atlantic off my native Irish Shores. It is one of the harshest places on earth to undertake such activities. The elements are against me right from the start; if something goes wrong, it's usually in an exposed, isolated, cold, often unknown location. It takes a deep desire to want to hunt and ride massive waves anywhere in the world, but here, in Ireland, where risk is at a premium, it takes a lifelong obsession to do it regularly and relatively safely. Major risks, unnecessary risks some might argue, and they would be right in some instances, but I believe I'm smart enough to know where I'm meant to be and where I'm not, and despite what I love to do, I argue that I'm relatively cautious. I'm extremely prepared, highly trained, extremely fit, knowledgeable, and experienced. All these things mean I know how to take calculated risks; I know when to go and when not to. That approach alone means I have control of myself and some of the elements which reduces fear and anxiety in the days leading up to a monster swell or in between pulses of open ocean surf as I sit out there waiting on the wave I want.

If you are reading this with no knowledge or interest in surfing, believe me, I also don't have much interest in the surfing scene. I don't know who is who, who has done what recently; I don't follow competitions or brands, and I literally couldn't care less. I'm only interested in what I do and what I want to do. This book isn't about surfing; it's about dealing with fear and anxiety and avoiding panic. It just so happens that big wave surfing is the thing that has taught me a lot about both it and myself. Think about a soldier who goes to war and comes back with a tale to tell about a specific battle. Or perhaps a round-the-world sailor who comes home with stories from the brink of disaster. Neither story drowns someone in over the top technicalities, but they illustrate points and pass on knowledge of certain situations and how they were dealt with. That's what this is. I'm not going to throw a load of cowabunga gnarly dude shakas and the like into it!

In fact, there is a lot more to me than big wave surfing, and this book illustrates some instances in other areas of life where fear has been present and dealt with because of what I have learned from my experiences in the sea.

I hope that anyone reading this can find a way to overcome whatever obstacles exist by whatever means is suitable to them. I believe there is no text book method as I know the things I do are very unique to me and to the situation.

Nothing and no one should stand in your way long enough to stop you achieving what you want in life, and that includes fear. If you can handle the fear, you can handle anything.

2

THE LIFESTYLE OF FEAR

Like anything in life, becoming efficient in handling fear takes practice. Your lifestyle can either be gripped by fear or your lifestyle grips fear, using it to move forward, not turn away. Some people are so downtrodden by the effect of turning away from trying things that they don't realise it has swamped their entire life and they have succumbed to it. They are beyond even realising that fear has taken control of them and overwhelmed their lives. It is possible to reverse that though if you put your mind to it and begin to make facing fear part of your everyday lifestyle until it becomes so normal that only the odd time do you realise that you are scared and must stop and think about how to proceed, if at all. I mentioned earlier how fear never completely goes away. It's the management of the fear which we can become proficient at and use in various walks of life if adapted to suit the various situations in which we find ourselves. I began surfing at the age of nine, and I gradually surfed increasingly bigger waves with very little guidance or input from others until I was a teenager, and even then, it was minimal. This meant that I was unknowingly becoming much more comfortable being uncomfortable in bigger and bigger surf, largely on my own. So, I was and still am continually putting myself in situations that scare me; in fact, the older and more experienced I get, the more scared I become, but that doesn't mean I stop pushing. I'm continually handling fear and moving forward, preventing panic setting in.

I've done this all my life, and it's overlapped and transferred into many other areas of my life. It has become a lifestyle for me, a normality to deal with fear and things that scare me along the way, but I never let it stop me. Yes, it might momentarily knock me off my track or path, but ultimately if I really want to do something, I will get through either with or without fear. And that is the thing to remember here – all of this is only relevant if you really want something. It's completely fine to turn around and walk away from whatever scares you if you don't want what is on the other side. There's no point going through anything you don't want to do just for the sake of it. In my experience, if this thing or experience or whatever it may be is something I really want to do, and it is just out of reach because I am scared, then I train myself to automatically deal with being scared and proceed anyway.

For me, dealing with fear is normal, I'm extremely used to it, and so it's not very often that it overwhelms me to the point of panic. For others, dealing with fear is something they have never done; they would turn from every situation without moving forward, and for that reason they may end up with less experiences, less opportunities, less stories to tell, less contentment. I mention stories because I am always the one with a story to tell; I have had so many experiences which would most likely never have happened had I not been able to deal with my fear at the time. Being aware of being scared but still able to march on has many positive knock-on effects in life in general which far outweigh the actual fear in the first place, or so it has been in my experience anyway.

If you are reading this, and you recognise yourself as someone who hasn't had many experiences because you have been scared and got into the habit of turning away at every opportunity because of that fear, then I really do believe you can learn something from me and what I have learned along the way. I am not a trained writer or Doctor of Psychology or someone that has studied to produce a report on fear, etc. I speak from pure first-hand experience in a specific field, quite often from fear of the unknown, to self-doubt, to extreme danger, fear of death, fear for others, and so on. I've been there and dealt with it. I deal with it and will always deal with it. So, know that what I have to share here is real; it comes from genuine first-hand experience and knowledge. I know the benefits of dealing with fear and anxiety and not letting it constrain my life and experiences. Dealing with it has given me huge confidence in who I am, my ability, and I know that I can roll with the punches, adapt and overcome, and when something happens, I will be at the front ready to deal with it. I am extremely fierce in my approach to most things in life, and often that approach is key in overcoming fear in the heat of the moment. However, I do not know the personal situations of anyone reading this, the depth of their knowledge, education, experiences, etc. I only know my own, and so I cannot advise on how to deal with fear in a specific situation, but I can explain and show how I have felt, its impact on me and others around me, and how I've dealt with it in various ways in the hope that it sparks something in someone's head and helps them devise a way to break through whatever it is they are worrying about.

Facing fear is a life-changing habit to form. Letting fear stop us is also life-changing. The presence of fear is good in some ways; I'm not saying it's a bad thing. Far from it. It stops us momentarily, makes us take check, assess, decide, move. It is a safety mechanism. It makes us re-think the current situation, decide if we have what it takes to proceed and allows us a moment to evaluate before deciding the next move. It gives us time to use rational logical thought before utter panic sets in and all control is lost. The key is to never reach panic. Being comfortable being uncomfortable and knowing I'm not ever going to allow myself into panic if possible, is key.

For example, a man in a forest has been chased by a lion to a river that he needs to cross. He can't swim. Fear stops him; he realises he needs to cross the river, but he can't swim, and it scares him, but he sees no immediate alternative. He is running out of time. Of course, he shouldn't attempt to swim the river if he can't swim. That would be plain stupid; he is dead right to be scared. He chooses to improvise and crosses the river another way further upstream. For me, I might get to the river and be concerned about current flow, the river bed, etc. I don't doubt my swimming ability, but the fear of these other unknown quantities stops me momentarily and allows me to assess the situation, and once I have decided if I think it's possible or not, I can make an educated decision and move based on that. I may decide to swim despite fearing the unknown quantities, but I base that on being confident that I will overcome whatever raises its head in the process. This is a much better alternative than being ripped apart by the lion. The other man's approach was different to mine based on our different skill sets and experience. We both cross the river; we just do it differently. Fear has stopped us both momentarily, allowed us to assess the situations, evaluate what we have to hand and mind and opened the door for a decision. The biggest difference to these two outcomes is that fear takes complete control because someone can't swim and stops them thinking properly, and they consider no other alternative because they are gripped with fear and panic sets in, so they never cross the river despite having other skills that they could draw on to cross it. Fear gripped them, froze them to the spot, and locked the mind in uncontrollable panic. They stay on the river bank motionless and give the lion a nice wee lunch. The fear of the water has been too much for them, and they can't for a moment think straight to cross it in any shape or form. It has a major impact on the rest of their life.

There are quite often so many alternatives to facing fear that people don't even realise the negative impact not facing fear has on them. People can easily fill their head with something else, fill their time with another lesser experience.

Becoming proficient in handling fear takes time; we never master it – it still has its moments over us, but working at dealing with it regularly makes it become normal behaviour, makes us aware and breathes life and confidence into us.

Everyone reading this is different. Some may have an overwhelming issue with fear of lots of things, lots of situations, etc., and some may be looking for answers to help deal with one thing – maybe its social, a public performance, more responsibility in work, issues at home, financial problems. It's different for everyone, so no one approach will suit every person or situation. For that reason, I know that lots of the material out there for people to learn something helpful from is not much use, but by reading other people's experiences, in this instance mine, I hope that whoever you are that something from what I've been through, done, and the ways I approach it may spark something inside you that will allow you to develop your own method of coping with it. Maybe everything I say helps; maybe only one minor detail that even I am completely unaware of being of significance to you helps. Whatever it is, I hope my experiences with fear and anxiety can help you in some way.

Look around you, who are your friends, who are your colleagues, who are your neighbours, your family? It is highly likely you are surrounded by people with a similar mindset to you in a lot of ways. Do most of them stay well within their limits? I bet the answer in nearly all cases is yes, and the reason I'm so confident of that is I see it plain as day. If you go into different neighbourhoods of the town or nearby towns, you will notice similar minded people live in the same area, do the same things, live very similar lives to each other. Not too many people have the balls to break the mould in their local clique; people are downtrodden by other less adventurous, less confident people, and if anyone dares step outside the confines of what is deemed acceptable or normal, they are ostracised. I have seen this first-hand on numerous occasions. People who appear not to be scared intimidate others. Most people don't have the balls to admit they are scared, and less have the balls to try and deal with it. So, when people see someone else as not scared, they cannot understand it and so close them out if not blatantly then subtly and over time. The thing that is missed here is that the person who appears to have no fear is most likely the most scared and has just grasped the thistle, taken the bull by the horns, and wrestled their way through it, and the benefits of doing so ooze from them.

If you find you have somehow become surrounded by these people with the inability or the desire to push themselves and drive forward, then it's going to make it even more difficult for you as you will feel pressure from them. I know you have experienced this, and finally you are starting to realise that your thinking has been right all along. You will leave people behind in being brave in the face of fear, not through you being a bad friend or whatever, but by taking on challenges and risks, you will suddenly have new experiences they cannot relate to, and you will begin to meet like-minded people who you can relate to and who can relate to you. They may not be in the same field as you, but they too will be proficient in dealing with fear, and you will share similar experiences. I don't have very many friends that surf; in fact, I can count them on one hand, and I have even less that surf big waves. Most of the people I would call my friends happen to be high achievers in various worlds, industries, and circles. They too will tell of stories where they felt people with less confidence, less drive to tackle their fears to reach their goals and dreams, attempted to pull them back. Eventually, they broke free, and they kept going, only bringing with them those who were not intimidated by their power of mind and newfound skill. This is the lifestyle of fear; it either works extremely negatively against you, or it works in your favour and enhances your life. Fear and the ability to deal with it can be the defining factor in living a happy and successful life ... or not. So, it's extremely important to educate yourself and find your own way to push through it as often as you can, or you will breed negativity to those around you, your children, or your spouse ... life will remain the same. Being able to challenge fears energizes people, breathes life into them, and brings new experience. It breeds confidence, new friends, opens new doors, and the more you push through fear, the better you get at it and fewer times in life will you feel trapped by it. You will never completely master it to the point of not being scared ever because it is there to protect us, let us pause, let us evaluate. It's supposed to be there, but it's not supposed to be a road block, a brick wall or cliff edge as it becomes in so many ways for us at various times in life. Being aware of it, knowing it should be there and not going into panic and freaking out over its presence is the key to attempting to deal with it.

I actively put myself in situations where I am scared; I have been doing it for a very long time and believe myself to be an expert in handling fear and can recall several instances when I have been scared but not panicked.

The thing about being able to overcome a fear in the heat of the moment is that the benefits are not just short-lived. The benefits cross over into all areas of life as you have now freed yourself of the anchor. Although the feeling of fear will never totally disappear, the next time you have to do the thing again it will be much easier knowing you have already been through this and come out the other side. That injection of strength carries over to other areas, and before long that mind trap you were in breaks down and you will be saying, "I am *insert name* ..." and I can do this!

The more you do it, the better life becomes. I know it may sound obvious, but it's true. Let me explain how it has led to me having the confidence in myself

31

to take on things I would never have thought possible.

When I was 22, my father died very suddenly. No warning signs, no build up. Here one minute, gone the next. Besides the obvious shock and hurt felt by all who were close to him, my ability to deal with fear and anxiety led me to do something that 24 hours earlier, I would never have known I was capable of. My father was a very successful house builder. He came from a background of at one time being a professional photographer, to a trawlerman, to a civil engineer, and then a house builder. In every sense of the word, he was a man. When he died, I didn't once hesitate in picking up his sword and continuing to fight on. I felt no fear; I felt no intimidation by what I was about to do. I took on his business of which I knew virtually nothing about. I only had experience of cleaning windows and floors in newly-built houses, marking out a couple of foundations, and a few other things. I had no idea what his plans were, what he had intended to do, or anything about the day-to-day running of a workforce of men twice my age with lifetimes of experience and knowledge on building sites. However, this did not scare me in the slightest. I fiercely charged on with complete confidence in my ability to adapt and roll with whatever I had to do to get through. Over the space of about six years, I oversaw the building of multiple housing developments of four-bed homes on greenfield sites including roads, planning permission, handling tradesmen, suppliers, purchasers, and even thieves. I jumped full head-first into the thick of it, and I solely put that down to my upbringing and my dad always standing by me as I pushed forward through my teens gaining experience in surfing and in other areas of life. I was always trying to push to the next level in everything I was doing throughout my childhood, and he always supported me. My parents never pushed me in any direction, they only ever assisted me and helped me have opportunities and allowed me to grow and go after things in life. Being able to deal with fear and anxiety has huge knock-on effects. It is naïve to think getting over the fear of one thing is the only reward of dealing with that fear. I sometimes go back to see all the houses and often wonder where I went in my head to pull that off! I do the same thing months after riding a huge wave when I see a picture of me at the bottom of a monstrous wave. It is amazing what the mind is capable of when it really wants something and is hell-bent on achieving it no matter what stands in its way.

3

LONE WOLF

It's January 14th. The ground is frozen solid below my almost see-through white wet feet. Its pitch black, windy, and raining. There is a slight glow coming out the side sliding door from the torch on my phone I propped up inside the van. I am on one of the most exposed headlands in Ireland, alone. I can hear the ocean roaring in the darkness. I'm convinced when the sun pokes its head up that the huge swell I have been tracking across the Atlantic will deliver the goods. I'm trying to get into my wetsuit which I have just pulled from eight inches of partially frozen water. I have never been one for hanging it up the night before; instead, it lies in a bucket in the back of my white transit freezing until the next day. I kind of like the pain; it kick-starts the fire.

I've spent the past hour peering into the inky darkness off the edge of the continent trying to see any sign of huge waves exploding in the distance. The fear of the unknown is running through my body, chilling me to the bone. I toss and turn all night long before these big swells.

I'm on my own today – no support team, no safety crew, no photographer, not even my dog is with me. No one could make it. Being alone is a good thing, it centres me, focusses me. As the light begins to break, reality sets in. The waves are huge. A rock lies in wait, just below the surface, ready to trip up these huge lines of swell which have marched their way across the North Atlantic for hundreds of miles. The waves stand tall and proud appearing invincible as they approach this isolated location only to be ambushed by the mysterious rock lurking in the icy, peat stained water. Their demise is imminent. They stop dead in their tracks, wobble, topple, fold at the waist and detonate with extreme violence into plumes of spray and vapour before settling back into the ocean. One by one, the army they marched with are slain in their path, big beautiful swell lines, brought to their knees. Spray drifts in the air like smoke from an exploded bomb. Everything I had been worrying about was justified at dawn. I've been doing this all my life, and the more I do it, the more I feel scared and worried. The more I do it, the more I am aware of the potential consequences of doing it.

I now have both bare white feet pulled through the legs of my dripping wetsuit. The stones on the ground are pushing deep into my almost numb feet. I stumble to where I kicked off my boots and stand on the discarded soles of them while I wriggle the wet freezing neoprene up to my waist. In doing so, I mutter under my breath, "Come on ya f£$%er." In one fell swoop, practiced and honed for a lifetime, I whip off all my six layers of T-shirts, sweaters, hoodie, coat and hat to bare my skin to the bitter wind. I slip one arm into my suit, then the next. I pull the zip up quickly, and I'm in! The soggy wetsuit boots are next before I get into my impact vests and helmet.

I slip one foot off the upturned boot and into a neoprene wetsuit boot. Incidentally, the left one has a hole in the sole. The light is almost up enough to see clearly. I know what I am about to explain is going to sound completely alien to almost anyone except about 30 people on this planet. The waves I am about to go out into are life-threatening. It's difficult to quantify these massive waves in measurements of feet or metres as so much more is relevant in their size and power, but I've often found analogies of swimming pools of water and waves as big as houses are lost on most people, and simple measurements work best. These waves are in excess of 30 feet. They aren't even that big, relatively speaking.

I walk to the back doors of my van and pull out three impact vests. I wear up to three impact vests when surfing on some big days. I slip the first one on, inside out. I wear it inside out to keep the buckles flush. I then slip the second on over the top of that. It has some stitching hanging out of it where I cut it open and filled it with some left-over foam to give me some more float in case I take a bad beating and get pushed ridiculously deep. I'm a big lad at 6'5" and 18 stone; most jackets aren't designed to float me, and they certainly aren't designed to bring someone up from 20 feet below a 40-foot wave. I pull out my third one. This one is homemade. It's a lycra vest with a chest panel of doubled up foam and a back panel of foam stitched into it. It kind of makes me look like a neoprene-clad superhero. It's always a struggle to get it on. Once I wriggle into it, I slip a red lycra vest over all the gear to keep it all fixed on as securely as possible. I've had some situations when I've been hit so violently by a breaking wave that impact vests have been ripped off over my head or their zippers and buckles have been blown open. I've had wetsuit boots sucked off my feet and wetsuits blown open by the power of the water exploding on me. The battle suit is on.

I reach up into the ceiling of my van. I don't have a kitted out camper van – it's an old transit. I don't have space for the luxury of a comfy bed, kitchen, and toilet in it. I have so much equipment that I need the bare shape of the van to get it all in. I keep as many big boards as I can in the ceiling tied up with old ropes and straps. I pull my pure white 12'6" from under another six boards of varying dimensions and place this on the ground with its nose under the van to stop the wind lifting it and blowing it across the rock. The board is about five inches thick and almost too wide to get my arm around.

I pull a ¾ used bar of wax from the same freezing bucket my suit was lying in. Optimistically, I begin trying to rub the rock-hard wax onto the board on top of old brown wax I just never got around to cleaning up and replacing. My hands are sharp with the cold, and my fingertips feel like ice. I toss the wax back inside the van, slam the doors, hide the key on the suspension spring, lift my board and begin to clamber down the rock face to the edge of the water.

The wind is howling offshore, and I'm carrying basically the wing of a plane under my arm. As I get below the top of the cliff face, I go into the wind shadow. Small stones are being blown off the top and down onto me as I scale the rock very carefully holding my board in my right arm and clinging onto the cliff face with neoprene clad fingertips. The first section is the sketchiest. There is some loose shingle here, but once I get down a few metres, I switch arms and turn the other way to traverse across the face of the cliff and down to the shore at an angle. Sometimes wild goats run up this path seemingly completely unaware of the potential death drop or the human carrying part of a plane under its arm.

I eventually make it to the water's edge. Large boulders are strewn across the shoreline, some as big as a car, some as small as a football. Waves are breaking just beyond the black rocks and rushing and crashing over them towards me. I'm trying to get into time with the surges and find a small window to clamber across the rocks and throw myself clear of them into the surf. I keep getting pushed back; the ocean is relentless this morning. I back up to below the cliff face to try and work out how I'm going to get through this shore break without being hurt or breaking my board. I decide to make a run for it during the next big set of waves, so that by the time it passes, I will be far enough out in the rocks that I will, all being well, get some time to throw myself into the surf and scramble out beyond the shore to break clear of danger. I start to make my way across the rocks, whitewater surging around me, trying to pull the board from my grip as I stand my ground among the boulders. Three waves have surged now, and I'm working my way through the rocks as each one draws out before the next surge. I'm blindly shoving my feet into holes between rocks and trying to get them back out before each surge comes. Eventually, there is a pause, and I clamber up and over the last few boulders banging the board on the rocks in the process as the water drains back out pulling me over the rocks and bouncing me in the process. I get my footing enough to launch myself and the board over the next surge and start to scramble out into the deeper water. I get my breath back and begin to paddle the one mile out to sea to where the submerged ledge of rock lies that is standing in the way of the huge swell and making the waves break. That's where I want to be.

As I stroke my way out to sea, completely alone except for the odd inquisitive gull swooping down on me, my heart is pumping with adrenaline. A low-lying sea mist fills the void between the reef and the land. I pause, paddling every now and again to check my position and to take a breather. The huge waves on the rock ledge are getting closer, the sound of them exploding getting louder, the coast getting further away. I let out a whoop of excitement and start to paddle again to get myself closer and into position.

I'm floating in the North Atlantic, a mile from shore. The only point of land I can see is a television mast on a mountain in the distance. At the same time as watching for approaching waves, I'm continually trying to establish my exact location based on the mast and the boils of water forced to the surface by the swells passing over the submerged rocks. I need to know precisely where I am, so I don't get caught but still be close enough to the danger zone to be able to catch one of these beasts. One moment of slack concentration and I could find I either get caught and beaten by a convoy of open ocean power or I miss the ride of my life. To catch one, I need to be positioned over the submerged rocks, but if I'm too close, I will get caught, and if I'm too far, I won't catch one. It's a balancing act. My heart is racing. I'm trying to keep my breathing regular, but the deep breaths and big exhales are making me over-think. My mind is in turmoil; I know I shouldn't be here, but I know I should be here. That's usually when I know I'm right in the spot to catch a bomb. A set appears on the horizon and begins to focus in on me. I can tell it's not big enough to break, but its energy is pulling me deeper into the submerged rocks, so I move myself away as it passes beneath me. As one approaches, it obscures my view of the next. I claw my way up the first huge dark moving wall of water. As I reach the top and get a vantage point, I see there isn't just one more, but I get a tiny glimpse of a third out the back. The offshore wind whips the top off the swell I'm atop, and as the wave passes beneath me unbroken, the airborne spray rains down on top of me, and the air fills with white mist. As the first passes, I drift down into the trough between it and the next. These are huge swells of water marching toward me, but they don't break as they aren't big enough to feel the submerged reef below and so pass on further towards shore, far in the distance. I claw over the next two, my heart beating fast with anticipation of what may be lurking behind the third that I might not have seen in that little glimpse I got from the top of the first one. Nothing, the ocean slips back into pause. I take a deep breath, or is it a sigh of relief? I'm never quite sure. This time waiting on these monsters to come is extremely stressful. I am far out at sea; I have virtually no points of reference except the mast in the distance that occasionally disappears as it is obscured by low-level cloud. It's a very lonely feeling, yet a very freeing feeling. I'm out here on my own, literally in the hands of Mother Nature.

The strong offshore wind is making the dark green water chatter against my 12'6 plain white surfboard as I sit astride it continually judging my position. I know a bomb is imminent. It's literally a matter of minutes before something frightening is coming my way, and I want to be in the right spot at the right time to ride it. Years of knowledge and experience are running through my veins with every beat of my heart as I try to stay one step ahead of the elements and be in the right place at the right time ready to wrestle my 12'6 onto one.

The horizon goes black. I know what this means. My initial feeling is to run for the safety of the deep water, but I sit tight. I'm not moving. I'm holding my ground this time. I take a glance over my shoulder for the mast on the hills to confirm my location; it's gone, obscured behind the cloud. I look for the rocks, and they are swirling with whitewater and gurgling, but I have no way of knowing where I am in relation to them without the mast. I switch to instinct. It's just me and the ocean now. I'm running on pure instinct at this point as the black horizon begins to march towards me. I can no longer feel my heart racing; I'm all in the mind now. There is an extremely unusual feeling of complete calm come over me in this moment; something I only experience when I know it's my time. I'm deathly calm; I'm not panicking, and I'm not fleeing. The set of monsters is getting closer; I sit astride my surfboard right in front of its path, and I'm not moving. It can come for me, hunt me down, but I'm not budging – I'm going to ride one of these.

As the first one approaches, I'm hoping I get a chance to let it pass by and give me an attempt at one of the bigger ones behind. The first one is approaching. A huge black wall of water is lining up as far to the west as it is to the east. It must get by me to detonate on the reef behind me. I scratch my way up the face of a 40-foot wall of moving water, and as I topple over the back of it, I take a quick glance down into the pit below me. The rocks are having all the water drawn from them in the vacuum between the wave and them. The wind is howling up the face towards me, blowing plumes of whitewater into the air. I mutter under my breath "f£$k" as I barely get over the top. Spray and wind howling everywhere around me as I paddle down the back of the beast and begin to see the next, even bigger one with me in its sights. I snap out of the victim mindset and quickly man the f£$k up. "Right you f£$£$n b£$£h it's on, let's go!" I grit my teeth, sit up on my board, slip to the tail, and swing it 180. The sound of the first wave exploding behind me is deafening, but I'm going. I'm now pointed towards the rocks, towards the wind, towards the chop, and this 40-foot beast from the deep is bearing down on me, closing in and about to blow me into oblivion. As I paddle, I take a quick glance over my right shoulder and then over my left. I adjust my line ever so slightly with a slightly deeper pull on my left side pulling me straight. Through gritted teeth, I growl, "Come on you f£$ker." I stroke hard as the wave stands tall on the reef, the rocks draining of water, the wind trying to lift the board from under me. I have my feet held up in the air as I paddle; my chin is almost flat on the board as I wrestle against the elements trying to get some forward momentum before standing on my feet. I'm almost vertical paddling the last couple of strokes, then bang, I'm up. I'm weightless. I feel no traction on the wave at all; the wind has got under my board, and I'm floating in the air momentarily. I have no feelings; I am all in the mind. The board tries to twist out from under my feet in the wind, turning slightly off axis, and then the tail and inside edge of the board catch on the face of the now completely vertical wave. The board pulls hard, and I manage to keep it under me as my weight drops onto it and both I and it start to slide down the wave. I'm compressed in what can only be described as survival stance. I'm trying to keep the board on an edge so as not to bury its nose into the bottom of the wave and be catapulted into hell. Finally, as I'm three-quarters of the way down it, everything is in flow. The board is planing well; I'm in a good position, and the wave is towering above me. I can now see the lines of current coming up the face of the reef and can feel the board chattering against the wind and chop, and I'm getting ready for the moment I've been waiting for. The chance at the very bottom of the wave to turn and lean into the bottom turn and get a good clear look at the beast hanging in the air above me as I harness all my speed and use it to propel me along the wave.

I look ahead and plan for placing the board on an edge within the curve of the wave. I slip the board onto its edge and compress down into the turn; my right hand touches the face of the wave as if to allow me to pivot around it. I glance up – towering above me, a dark wall of water capped with a feathered white lip is hanging in the air about to throw out and take me out. I lean into the turn and drive the board off the bottom and across the wave; the falling white lip detonates behind me sending an explosion of whitewater out and all around me. My board begins to cavitate in the oxygenated water, but its long low rail grips in the green solid wave and pulls me straight. I'm in full survival stance now. Hunkered down low, arms out straight, spray and froth everywhere, but my speed from the bottom turn projects me out of the path of the wave and into the deep-water channel. I let out a huge whoop and collapse into the water filled with adrenaline, excitement, relief, and achievement. I'm literally on fire. My mind is going Mach ten, as is my heart. That is the few seconds all this is for. The few seconds of complete calmness in the moment where only instinct controls and allows for the flow of everything into the body and mind to be processed at super high speed to perform. I imagine the experience is like riding a bull! I came out here for that experience; sometimes it doesn't go as fluid as that – sometimes it goes horrifically wrong. I know I got as good a ride as I will get out there, so I call it quits, minimise the risk, and paddle back to shore ecstatic!

I'm not suggesting everyone should start surfing big waves! For me, facing the fear and anxiety associated with big wave surfing has taught me some valuable lessons. Everyone has something which scares them to the point they don't do it despite wanting to. It's a different thing if you don't want to do something and are also scared. But when it's something you want to do, and fear holds you back, that is truly devastating.

My experiences with dealing with fear and anxiety from an early age in the surf and later in competition have 100% benefited me in many other ways in life. I have done things along the way that I literally took the same approach I have always done with surfing.

Over the years, with increasing danger, bigger waves, more isolated locations, pioneering missions into the unknown, I've scaled everything up. Boards are bigger, thicker, and heavier; I'm bigger, thicker, and heavier for that matter! Wetsuits are warmer and more flexible. I wear not one, not two, but three specially crafted lifejackets at times over my wetsuit, and over all that I wear a Lycra vest tied at the waist to keep everything on during extreme impacts and violence when I fall or get caught by a big wave. At least if I go unconscious underwater, I will surface.

Big wave surfing involves extreme management of risk, fear, and anxiety. Later in this book, I explain in more detail how I go about managing these things to allow me the opportunity to surf some of the biggest waves on the planet.

4

WITNESSING FEAR AND PANIC

I recently witnessed a close friend experience extreme fear. I took this guy to a surf spot he had never been to before. A very dangerous spot with shallow water and rocks on an exposed headland. It was a beautiful, sunny winter's day, no one around, just four of us who had come together to surf this day. The night before he texted me joking about being scared and asking me questions about how big it would be. I am fortunate to have been through the fear thing so many times in big waves that I was able to tell him he would only be scared beforehand, not in the moment.

When we eventually paddled out to the spot, everyone else got waves within the first five minutes except him. It was scary, breaking very close to the rocks and obviously dangerous. He was well within his rights to be intimidated and scared. Every time a set of waves approached, he would try and paddle for the edge of one of them hoping he could sneak onto the wave without too much hassle and without having to go and sit in the scary bit where the wave was steepest and breaking violently into waist deep water over a rocky ledge. In the next half an hour he froze up, not cold, but in fear. He had completely drained himself of energy with the worry and fright that he was now just sitting there staring, wide-eyed at the horizon. Every time a set approached, he scrambled out of the way. I told him where he needed to sit; he already knew deep down where he needed to put himself to catch a wave, but he didn't really want to, but at the same time he did! Conflicting messages inside the head were making it impossible for him. I told him to shadow me and reassured him that once he did this he wouldn't be scared while he was on the wave, just before. I called him into a few waves, but he didn't really commit. The waves were fast moving and standing up abruptly at the very last minute making surfing them very technical. He would paddle and pull back, or paddle slightly out of the way so as not to catch the wave but was hopeful he might get lucky. He was sitting hunched over, clearly deep in thought, but if I'm correct, with a blank mind. Staring out to sea, in a daze. I tried repeatedly to get him to be in the exact position required, but it just didn't happen. He even got hammered a few times, and that didn't even blow the cobwebs off enough to let him push himself over the ledge and into one. Eventually, the tide got really low, and it was getting dangerous with rocks now jutting out of the water in places. I decided I was going to paddle in as I was on a 10-foot board that wasn't really built for the steep waves, and I didn't want to break it. He decided to stay in for a little longer and try again. I paddled all the way back to shore, and as I climbed up the rocks and up to where I could get a look out to the waves, I saw him go on one, a decent sized wave. He stood up and rode the wave with no problems. A short intense ride! I let out a hoot and punched my fist in the air above my head in support! That one wave broke the fear, and he paddled back out again and went on another wave within a few minutes! He called it a day and came ashore. The difference between his mood and demeanour from when I was sitting out at sea with him to when he was ashore was like night and day. In the water, he was all hunched over, static, uptight, wide-eyed and frozen. By the time he had come ashore, he was grinning ear to ear, loosened up, walking proud and clearly feeling really at ease and pleased with himself! He went through hell. It started 24 hours in advance; he didn't sleep. He then went out there and froze up, terrified, staring blankly out to sea, and he was overcome by fear. He eventually overcame it and achieved not only catching some of the scariest waves of his life, but he overcame the challenge of dealing with paralyzing fear and achieving his goals. That's what it's all about – he freed himself, and it changed his entire outlook, his energy, and happiness. That's how it is for me too every time I break my way through being scared; it is like a relief, and suddenly, the stress and negativity leave the body and mind, and I feel great.

5

DISCONNECTED

It was 2008. I was about to paddle out from the headland at Mullaghmore Head on the west coast of Ireland on my nine-foot surfboard on a big wild, windswept day. There were two tow teams in the water, but I was adamant I wanted to paddle. For anyone who doesn't know, tow teams use jet skis to tow a surfer into the path of a big wave like a water skier behind a boat, and then the surfer lets the rope go and surfs the wave. It is a major advantage in certain conditions and locations. I do paddle into big waves with arm power alone like lots of others do too, and I also tow surf, but on this day, I was paddling. My friend had come from Portrush with

59

me and another two guys from Portrush were there too. The other two guys were completely out of their depth. They jumped off the headland on tiny shortboards and began to paddle out. They clearly had no idea what they were doing or had any idea of how big and violent the surf was this day. 40-foot monsters were exploding in wild winds. They ended up paddling way out into the bay in a position that they were more vulnerable to not getting back ashore because of the winds than they ever were at getting close to a breaking wave. They were clearly out of their depth, and thankfully, they knew it and not too long later went back ashore. The tow-in guys were getting waves as my friend and I paddled out. Incidentally, neither of us was wearing any floatation vests at the time. I wasn't feeling overly scared this day, but it was my friend's first time out there, and he was clearly frightened. We both narrowly avoided getting murdered by a huge wave that we both just scraped up over the face of as it rushed past us like a freight train over the reef. We weren't so fortunate with the next one. It started to explode on the exposed rocks to the south-west, and we knew its main peak was just in front of us as it started to wall up all along the rock ledge just under the water and ahead of us. We were scrambling as fast as we could to the north to try and get out of its way, but our efforts were of no use. The huge brown wave stood up on the rock ledge, took aim, and detonated right in front of us. We got annihilated. I was under water spinning around and around going deeper and deeper hoping I wasn't going to bump into my friend and get tangled. Soon my leash tightened, and I started to swim back up to the surface. As soon as I popped up, he was nowhere to be seen, no board, and no sign of him. Then his board shot up out of the water, but he wasn't attached to it. I assumed his leash broke. A few seconds later, he popped up and took a huge gasp for air. I immediately burst out laughing at us. He was not impressed. It really scared him to the point he panicked underwater and made the decision to remove himself from his board. Thankfully, there wasn't another wave directly behind it, and he had plenty of time to settle down. Like a true warrior, he calmed himself down and made his way back out to the peak of the reef alongside me. I caught three waves that day, two of which I got steamrollered by huge whitewater and the other I rode successfully, but he also caught three waves despite this being his first time, getting a serious beating and panicking. I was really pleased for him. It must be said, he is one of the most competent surfers I know, and it was only a matter of time before he was catching bombs at Mullaghmore. He went through the mill and came out the other side. That's what it's all about!

6

1OOFT NAZARE

I was sitting outside a fish factory in a little town in Ireland called Tuam. I had received an email from a guy who had an old jet ski he wanted me to have as he felt I could do more with it than the life it currently had sat on a pallet in the back of his factory, so I went down to collect it. A very kind and generous thought, and I even left with a side of salmon for my mum! I was just pulling out of his yard when the phone rang. It was an American mobile number, and I immediately knew it was Garrett McNamara. Garrett is an excellent big wave surfer, and he had come to Europe to focus on surfing the big waves that break at Nazare Portugal. I had been working with him and a crowd of others down there any time a big swell arrived. He called me this day to tell me that the swell forecast was likely to produce the 100ft waves we had been waiting for. Nazare has extremely unique bathymetry which magnifies an average-sized swell into a gigantic-sized swell in certain conditions. He asked if I could go and meet him there and tackle the peak of the swell. I explained I was on my way to Co. Clare to appear in a new advert for the Irish tourist board, and once I was finished doing that I would fly from Belfast to Lisbon for the swell. He told me to bring extra floatation this time, and he needed to borrow one of my tow board fins because he had lost his last one. He explained to me that if this came off then the media from it would go bananas. I took that as meaning he had no doubt that this was the swell of a lifetime. When I put the phone down and started driving, I was thinking about what a 100-foot wave was going to look like. I had ridden waves that were probably 50-60 foot at Nazare at this point, so I knew its power and energy well, but this was going to be most likely the biggest swell ever ridden in the history of surfing. I was driving out of Tuam looking at the street lights. Normally, I drive along envisaging huge walls of water lined up down the side of the street, the same size as the top of the street lights, and I envisage myself surfing them. This time I was driving along trying to do the same but doubling the height of the street lights. It was a crazy experience. All my life, I had been making the calls for people to come with me because there were huge waves coming, and I wanted someone to come play with me; this was the first time it had ever been the other way around where someone had called me to tell me to come away from my shores to another country in pursuit of the biggest waves in the world. Don't get me wrong, I've travelled the world surfing big waves, but to be going to someone else's project was alien to me, and now a couple of winters down the line at Nazare, and we are looking at potentially the biggest waves ever ridden on their way. Even for us seasoned big wave riders, that's a crazy thought; in fact, it may be a crazier thought for us than for onlookers because we know the consequences and the drama, the feelings, and emotions that can and do unfold more than anyone. It was probably a good thing I had a couple of days filming at the Cliffs of Moher to get through before the arrival of the swell as it kept my mind occupied.

I flew down to Nazare and put in a training day in preparation for the big day. Every wave I rode I was trying to visualize it being three times as big, and every time I fell and was being collected by the jet ski I was pretending to myself the whitewater chasing behind was huge. I was trying to prepare myself in advance by thinking of all the different scenarios which may unfold the next morning to be one step ahead in my mind. That night, the team of Portuguese local men looking after the skis was making sure everything was OK for everyone going on the water the next day. They were even trying to rig a huge rope with a handle on the end of it so if something bad happened and a fallen surfer couldn't be rescued from the sea, maybe the rope with the handle could be of some use from a height. Serious measures were being thought of ahead of what was expected to be the biggest surf ever ridden.

I spent that night mostly awake wondering and thinking about everything; I should have been sleeping, but I rarely sleep. I am usually too anxious and running everything through my head repeatedly.

The morning came, and I was up before first light to get ready. The biggest waves ever ridden had not materialized. All the stress, anxiety, and commitment suddenly seemed to be nothing but overhype and now tiredness. There were still huge waves, and I was lucky enough to ride a few of the biggest waves of my life that morning in beautiful sunny weather far from what I was used to back home. It appeared that the giant swell was a little later to arrive than previously thought, and it looked like it was going to arrive in the night or by dawn. However, what happened next was something that I remember more vividly than almost anything else.

.... I was lying in my bed in an apartment just above the out of season cobbled whitewashed main street of Nazare. It was 1.30 a.m., and the room was pitch black as the plastic roller shutters on the windows were closed so tight. The bed was a single pine framed one with a headboard and another bit of wood along its foot. I hate those beds cos I am so tall I usually hang my feet over the end, but that thing gets in the way, so I never really sleep properly, and before such a big swell, it would be best to get some sleep!

The apartment was on the second floor, probably about a mile away from the lighthouse at Praia do Norte where these huge waves break and maybe half a mile away from the town beach on the southern side of the headland. I was tossing and turning thinking about the morning and what I was going to face. Although I regularly surf huge waves, I always get anxious beforehand, especially the night before. I nonstop ponder, worry, think, examine, check all night until I eventually fall asleep no doubt from exhausting myself. I have become more relaxed about it over the years through repetition, but I still stress myself out a little at times as I know I am never too far from a serious incident if I am not paying attention to a lot of finer details.

I really couldn't sleep; on top of all that the bed was doing my head in! I just couldn't get comfortable, and it was starting to piss me off. Every time I moved, I noticed the bedroom door that was closed tight would rattle a little and the bedside table too. I kept tossing and turning and then I would be lying there still in the darkness and hear the door rattle and the bedside table too. It would happen for a second or two and then back to silence. At first, I put it down to my movement causing it, and then when I kept hearing it repeatedly every few minutes, I started to really listen hard trying to work out what was causing it. To my utter shock, I realised it was the waves detonating on either the shore break or the rocks at the headland. They were exploding with such force they were sending shock waves and causing both the bedside table and the door to tremble ever so slightly in the darkness of the room. Do you know when you think you heard a noise at night and you then lie there dead still with nothing moving except your eyeballs as you try to listen? That's what I was doing. I had never experienced anything like this. I then started to wonder what on earth must the surf be like if this is happening? My mind was running wild; I wasn't sure if I should be excited or terrified. This rattling was new to me. I had spent many nights in Nazare at this point, surfed some gigantic waves, and yet I had never heard this rattling. I knew that the next morning was going to be like nothing else I had experienced and probably like nothing else the surfing world had ever seen before. The anticipation was off the chart.

As daylight broke, lines stacked far out to sea groomed by an offshore wind filled the dawn view from the lighthouse at Nazare.

It's almost impossible to get out there from the beach itself, so we took jet skis from the harbour and drove north towards Praia do Norte. Four of us motored out on three jet skis being watched over by Nicole, Jorge, Wilson, Paulo, and a few others on the headland with radio connection to us giving us eyes in the back of our heads so to speak as they could alert or warn us of things we may not have seen. The plan was as always to rotate between safety driving, surfing, towing, keeping extra gear safe. Three skis allowed us the ability to have a lot more equipment and confidence in huge seas, and if something happened, we would have several chances to put it right. Just the day before Garrett had come in to rescue me in huge whitewater, and as we raced back out we got caught by a big close out right in the lip of the wave, capsized, and lost the ski. I went over the falls with the wave whilst still on the rescue sled. It all happened so quickly I didn't get a chance to get away from the ski so just got thrown over the falls with it. Losing jet skis in big surf is unfortunately a very common thing, and something which is unavoidable at times. So, we ideally have a minimum of two skis on the water in any big tow surf session anywhere in the world, but on this day, we took three.

There is a huge towering overhanging cliff at Nazare, and I often envisaged it to be the size of the waves that may one day come in here. On this day as I drove towards the cliff, along the edge of the town beach, I really thought this may be the day that it became reality. Waves were exploding up over the rocks that lie just off the lighthouse. Those rocks are 40 feet tall, and the waves were exploding over them like they were pebbles on the beach. It was gigantic. Huge teepee shaped walls of water were toppling into the bay one after another with virtually no pause and certainly no care that anyone wanted to try and ride them.

In the days before, I had been surfing a new tow board, and I had a nerve-wracking experience when I got to the bottom of an average-sized wave and the board I was riding slipped out from under me and lost grip on the surface making me fall. It only happened once, but I knew it was an issue with the board design when I specifically went on left-handers. So, I had decided not to go on any lefts for fear of falling badly, but on this morning, the biggest waves were left-handers. I had adamantly told myself I was not going to go on lefts, but I was not going to miss the opportunity to ride some truly huge waves. When it was my turn to surf, Garrett got me up on the rope, and a wave swung in towards the lighthouse headland. I was nervous and didn't really want to go, but I made my mind up, and as Garrett swung me into position, I let go of the rope and started hurtling down the face of the thing. As I dropped down the face, in my right eye I could sense the cliff getting closer and closer and then the detonation of the whitewater exploding out past me; in my left eye, the large dark blue wall of water towered up above me, and in the distance, the golden sandy beach. All this information and sights coming at my senses at a million miles an hour as I continued down the huge peak. Most of the waves at Nazare don't have a defined bottom to them where it's possible to spot where to put a bottom turn in and propel myself back up the face of the wave. Mullaghmore for example is a much steeper, ledge type of wave, and that allows placement of a bottom turn whereas Nazare requires a different approach to get down the wave far enough to gather speed but not too far to not have enough speed to outrun the avalanche of whitewater coming behind. I rode the wave successfully and pulled out over the shoulder, and Garrett came to get me. It wasn't as big as was hoped; my wave was big and felt great, but it wasn't the 100-footers expected. However, there was a distinct higher level of energy in the water this morning. It felt alive, more so than normal. Garrett decided he was going to go on a wave and slipped into the water. I rotated onto the safety ski and drove inside a little further towards the headland to get a better vantage point to watch over him. As if it was meant to be, three huge peaks appeared within minutes of him slipping into the water. I positioned myself as best I could to watch as he was driven into their path letting go of the rope and heading down into the centre of one of the incredible blue peaks. I will never forget the sight of him leaning on his board charging straight down the unbroken mountain of water heading straight into its bottom. I was sure this was the biggest wave ever ridden. It was ridiculous. The thing was like a hillside moving through the water which then toppled and sent a massive avalanche of whitewater down after him. He outran it and successfully rode the beast. It was an incredible sight, and strangely those three waves were the only ones of that size that came through all morning. It was his day; it was meant to be. The sky was blue and the sea smooth. Upon arrival back at the harbour, it was clear from the applause and crowd gathering that the wave he rode was most likely the biggest ever surfed. Once I saw the pictures later that day that Wilson Ribeiro had taken, it was mind-blowing. I wrote an article on my website at the time that went viral. I told this story and the experience from my point of view on the ski watching over him. Before long, media channels from all over the globe were on the story, and the wave was measured by various people as anywhere from 70 feet to 104 feet. No one could agree on its exact size. In my opinion, I had the best vantage point from the safety ski as I was ringside, so to speak, and I estimated it to be 90 feet. The world went mental. It was headline news in almost every country and resulted in a Guinness World Record.

These sorts of things do not happen with fear not being present, the fear is always present in varying degrees, but it is the keeping going regardless and adapting that makes humans able to do things which at some points in time appear beyond humanly possible. Big wave riders are continually pushing personal boundaries as well as sporting boundaries with every new storm that sends waves to our shores. Big wave riders are the few men and even fewer women who have the combination of desire, passion, and ability to put themselves in harm's way to chase life-threatening waves where consequences run high. The price to pay can be fatal, but the memories and the stories created are all worth the wrestle and tussle with our biggest opponent, fear!

7

LESSONS LEARNED IN FEAR CROSSOVER TO OTHER AREAS OF LIFE

Sometimes we must move and think quickly; something happens very suddenly, and we have had no time to prepare or plan for dealing with this. If we are lucky, the thing that causes immediate fear or anxiety might be something we have experience of or skills in, and we will get a grip of it quickly. Other times, we don't have that luxury and must think and move fast to deal with it or panic fills in and consumes us. There are lots of examples of this in my life, not just in surfing, and I know that many people reading this can relate to some of these examples more easily than the surfing stuff. In fact, it's probably true to say I have become, as most big wave surfers have, expert in handling fear relating to surfing big waves through continued exposure to it, making us increasingly more comfortable. The skills of thinking quickly and absorbing information on the move are transferable to other areas in life which means being panicked is extremely rare. I must admit at times fear does get the better of me, and sometimes I will pull back on a big wave at the very last second not committing because I am scared, and in other walks of life, fear and anxiety do raise their heads. Sometimes I'm able to deal with them well and others I muddle through. I have a very good awareness of their presence so that means I probably have a better chance of dealing with them than most. I imagine the same is true for anyone exposed regularly to something scary. Police officers must become adept at dealing with fear in confrontational situations and rarely, if ever, panic. When fear and anxiety come on quickly, it can be extra terrifying and extremely overwhelming, making it difficult to keep a cool head.

The following are a few instances in which I have experienced fear in other areas of my life. I believe some of the skills came directly from continued exposure to fear in the ocean.

8

BURGLAR

I was asleep in the house on my own aged 22. It was a winter night, and we lived in the country, far from street lights or much traffic on the lane next to the house. We'd had a few instances over the years of burglaries and attempted burglaries, so we had security lights all around the house. There was an alarm which allowed us to be in the house and zone other areas off and have them alarmed. I was in the house on my own this night as I regularly was. At approximately 1.30 a.m., my mobile phone began ringing. It was sitting on my bedside table in front of the only light in the pitch-black room that was coming from my radio alarm clock which showed the given time. To be honest, I was sleeping deeply, and I didn't realise the phone was actually ringing for a moment or two, and then I suddenly came around somewhat and saw that the number on the screen that was calling was from the alarm monitoring company in Belfast. I thought *that's weird*, so I answered it. The lady on the phone told me to get to the house because their system was telling them that the alarm was ringing which meant there must be a break in. She also said they had already informed the police, and they are on their way. I told her she was wrong, and that there must be something wrong with their system because the alarm wasn't ringing. She was adamant that it was ringing, and I tried to reassure her that I was already in the house and that's how I knew. Then suddenly, I came to and realised I could hear the alarm, and I just wasn't awake enough for the first minute or two! I confirmed with her that she was correct and put the phone down. Immediately, I filled with fear. I didn't know how long this was ringing for before I noticed; I didn't know who had broken in, how many of them there were, and what they were after! I was thinking fast trying to work out what I was going to do. I knew the police were on their way, so if I had to deal with something, at least I would have back-up soon. Our house was a big sprawling bungalow. Someone could have got in in several places and I wouldn't know, but before I went to bed at night, I always closed the glass hall door exactly for this scenario as I knew if someone got in at least I would have an idea if they had crossed that line in the sand. I decided I was going to check and see if that door had been moved. I stayed below the window sill in my room despite the curtains being shut because there was a huge full moon shining, and I didn't want any chance of anyone who may be outside seeing me move. I crept over to the door which went into a little bathroom that linked my room with my wee brother's room. I gently slid the door open hoping no one was behind it. The only sound I could hear was my breathing. It was dead silent. I slid along the bathroom floor on my bare knees and listened on the other side of the next door which was into his empty bedroom. There was a lot of light shining below the door but not enough to be a ceiling light. I realised it was the moon, and it was shining through his window that had no curtains pulled because he wasn't there. I knew if I got this door open and into his bedroom I could get to the hall from his room. I would be right next to the glass hall door if I opened his main bedroom door. I quietly pulled the door handle down hoping it wouldn't creak and crept into the room on my belly, commando crawling across the floor below the moonlight coming through the window. It was like daylight; it was so bright outside. I tried to have a look out the window up towards the trees on the bank outside to see if I could see any vehicles that shouldn't be there. I crept to the back of his door which led to the hall. From there, once opened, I would be able to see the glass door. I was really hoping no one was in the hall. I was completely unsure of what I was going to be confronted with upon opening the door. I listened as hard as I could but heard nothing. Then a huge bang in the distance. *F£$k*, I muttered to myself. I crept the door handle down and quietly and slowly opened the door. There was no one there. The house appeared to be in darkness and silent. I sneaked my head around the doorframe to get a look through the glass door, and there was no light that way either, but the reflection off the glass was obscuring my view. I knew I had to go through that door now. Previously someone had forced entry into my parents' room at the opposite end of the hall, but they had a wooden creaky floor, so I figured if someone was there I would have heard them. I had to go through this door, and I had to go now. Again, all I could hear was my fast breathing, but I knew I had to defend this place. I slid up off the floor and stood against the wall and the doorframe trying to get a clear view out one of the hall windows to the other side of the house where I could see the back doors and windows in the moonlight; nothing seemed disturbed. I decided to go for it. I abruptly walked out of the room into the hall, snatched the door handles on the double glass hall door and began moving through the house loudly and aggressively, turning on every light as I went. Next, I saw flashing lights coming through the windows as I went, so I knew I had back-up. I kept going, expecting to come across someone or a sign that someone was there until I got to the back door and opened it to the police. They came in, and we went through the house checking all windows, doors, and potential hiding places and found nothing. Not even a mark or a sign of an attempt. I was really confused. I was woken from my sleep very suddenly, and then I had this immediate situation to handle and was completely in the dark as to what was going on. I was scared, and now this. I realised later I dealt with the fear by quickly trying to establish what was going on and trying to work out where was safe and where was not. I unknowingly calmed the situation by trying to quickly educate myself on the safest places and potential points of entry, and once I had done that, I attempted to face whatever was there. Nothing was found that night by the police or me, but a couple of days later, I discovered some of the hedges and trees at the back of the house had been disturbed. I can only describe it as looking like someone who didn't know where they were going had pulled and hauled their way through the undergrowth leaving an obvious mark and trail. I assume somewhere around the house, and I still don't know where, whoever the trespasser was, attempted to get into the house that night and the alarm picked them up before they actually broke in. Maybe they tried to force a window frame, or a door, and it was enough to trigger the alarm, but they left no marks on the frames. I also still don't know what the bang was, but they clearly did enough to set the alarm off after wrecking their way through the trees and hedge. Thankfully, I didn't have to deal with whoever that was, and it ended up being a learning experience about myself and dealing with fear and keeping going regardless.

9

BAR

I am so rarely in bars; I really dislike bars and quite often find someone is being a dick, and I have zero tolerance, so I just don't enjoy myself there. It's just not for me. As a teenager in bars, etc., I sometimes found someone wanted to try and fight with me. You would be forgiven for thinking me being bigger than most people would be a deterrent, but it appeared to make me stick out, and I think possibly seen as a challenge for someone in front of their mates. It resulted in a few scuffles over the years, but nothing too major. However, more recently, I was in a bar and with some friends in a little area by a fireplace. The fire roared in the corner continually being stoked by the young barman. I immediately noticed a guy on the opposite side of the room. I have always sensed a bit of an attitude from him, so I am always keeping an eye on him when he is around. Anyway, I just had a feeling something was going to happen with him, so I positioned my stool in a way that I could see him clearly without looking at him directly. I was on a little low barstool, and he was sat further into the room on a bench at a table. While I sat there chatting and carrying on with my mates, I could see every now and again in the corner of my eye that he was peeking around people and menacingly looking over at me. I didn't know what he was up to, but it concerned me. After a while, he got up out of his seat and was clearly getting ready to leave. I knew if something was going to happen now he had been planning it based on where I was sitting. I was watching everything he was doing, but at the same time continuing to chat to my mates, so he didn't know I was paying any attention to him. I didn't want to make eye contact and start him getting arsey, I just hoped he would get bored and stop it. As he approached, I slid the stool out of his way and said hello. He slid by but didn't respond right away. To be honest, I was in a vulnerable position sitting down if he was to try anything, and I probably should have stood up. He slid past, and then as soon as he was by me, he turned around and put his hand out to shake mine and said, "Big Al." I looked up at him and shook his hand, momentarily thinking I had been unduly concerned. I was wrong, he began to try and pull me up off the stool whilst repeatedly shouting "Big Al" at me. He gripped my hand and was attempting not to let go. I was thinking *ffs here we go* but I immediately knew what I was going to do; I didn't even hesitate or have a second thought about it. I didn't want to make a scene, but at the same time, I wasn't going to let him escalate this. He pulled the first time and caught me slightly off guard, so I based myself. He then pulled the second time to which he had a bit more resistance from me, and I settled back onto the stool; the third time was go time! He yanked with all his might and again shouted "Big Al!" In a split second, I used my left thumb over his hand and forced the lower part of his right thumb back up under the upper part. It's difficult to explain what I

89

did, but it basically renders the hand grip useless, and because he was pulling so hard and had no grip and was no longer attached to my weight, he went flying backwards, out the open doorway, across the corridor, and hit the wall! He was completely shocked. He went from being a cocky dickhead to stunned. I continued to sit on the stool, and only a couple of people noticed the commotion but didn't see exactly what had happened. I could see he was momentarily thinking of charging into the room again at me, and then in the same second, he glazed over, froze to the spot, and stared through me as if I wasn't there. He reached for the zipper on his jacket and began to do it up before walking away! I was not expecting it to end that quickly and was relieved when he walked off! The last thing I needed was a row in a bar! He tried to intimidate me all night in that room, but I didn't give him any acknowledgement. He was clearly ruining my night because I couldn't relax, anxious that something was going to happen, so I was trying to stay ready instead of relaxing with my mates. He had put this fear over me all night, and all I could do was stay alert. It ended up that the fear he tried to instill was thrown back into him in a split second of quick thinking, and he finished up frozen to the spot probably wondering what just happened and what was coming next! He tried to use fear and intimidation then was escalating it to violence because he was getting frustrated at the lack of reaction, which is when I struck and disrupted his train of thought without doing him any harm but making him realise he was not in control and becoming fearful of what might come next. He had given me lots of opportunity to deal with the fear he was trying to instill in me. I was able to watch him, and realise he was leading up to something. He was drinking, and I knew he only had one mate. I had lots of information which controlled the fear, which gave me the upper hand. In a split second, I turned it all on him. I didn't give him any opportunity to prepare, and I led him to believe I didn't know he was sneakily trying to start something, so I caught him off guard with my reaction which left him shocked and scared and ultimately de-escalated the situation very quickly. I was lucky it ended like that!

I'm not one to get into physical altercations; it doesn't matter how well trained someone is in any sort of martial art or fighting system, things never go to plan, and usually both parties get injured. I have a triple black belt in Krav Maga, and I've been teaching it too for years, but that does not mean I would ever want to get into any sort of fight. If anything, it makes me more fearful of those situations, and so I always try to avoid any sort of physical confrontation. I think in lots of ways, martial arts training can lead to a false sense of security for people, and it's not until some real experience is gained that real confidence comes out from that training. I'm sure everyone reading this can relate to having the jitters and panicking in moments of confrontation that have come on very quickly. We get no time to prepare for that in those situations, and sometimes all training and plans go out the window, and we flap and behave in ways we never expected despite lots of training. Fear takes over rational, well-trained minds on a regular basis in all walks of life and it can be shocking for the person it happens to and leave them very confused as to why after all the years of training that they flapped in the moment of confrontation. The feelings and emotions that come in those moments are virtually impossible to train for, for most people unless in the military or police, for example, and so they come out of nowhere at times and catch us off guard.

10

BUNGIE JUMP

It's 8 a.m., and I am in a minibus with four surfers from around the world and a national TV crew. We are on our way from Jeffrey's Bay in South Africa to the biggest bungie jump in the world. We were filming a two-part series for a tv show after we had all been finalists in a surf competition that toured the UK and Ireland. I had finished second overall. The TV crew wanted some extra content for the show so took us to this huge gorge with a concrete road bridge spanning it. One of the guys opted not to do the jump for medical reasons.

I had never considered a bungie jump before; it was not something that ever interested me, and I was nervous about it, but I hadn't really been thinking too much. I was more concerned if we would make it back to the beach in time for a surf before dark.

The minibus pulled into this stoned car park with nothing there except a little wooden hut peeking out of the cloud resting on top of the hill. The world's biggest bungie jump wording on a sign just above the door. It was an eerie scene. Foggy cloud drifting around, and this little hut standing on its own. Then out came the guide. He was a big, well-built guy, the climber looking sort, probably never too far from a bag of chalk and a carabiner kind of look about him! He brought us in and gave us a quick chat before leading us over to the bridge. The silence was broken by the noise of cars and lorries rushing over the join between the road and the bridge. Thud, thud, thud, thud, thud, thud, over and over again. I assumed we were going to walk out the bridge next to the road, but to my surprise, he led us to a metal gate below the bridge. This gate was the opening at the end of a completely enclosed steel gangway that hung below the towering bridge over the deep scar in the hillside into which we were about to throw ourselves attached to a big rubber band!

I was at the back of the line behind the other surfers and the film crew. As I walked in, the door swung on a self-closer mechanism and slammed shut behind me, rattling the steel cage. We were then walking along a steel mesh floor, and with every step we were getting further out under the bridge and further out above the gorge. We were getting higher and higher, the thud, thud, thud, thud, still going on above us. The guide was walking backwards, and because he was about the same height as me, he could see me clearly all the way across the others' heads. I must have looked concerned as he called me forward to the front and got me to walk in front of everyone else close to him. The walk took a few minutes, and we exited the steel cage out onto the concrete beams that were supporting the bridge across the opening. Above us was the road and under foot bright grey concrete with a steel handrail along the edge forming a little bay to jump from. There was a CD player there, and everyone got the opportunity to play music to jump to. Paul, the cameraman was loving this! He had previously worked at a jump in another country and so was rigged up and hanging off the side of the bridge as if there was not a huge drop below him. He had the camera on his shoulder, ready to shoot the jumpers! I was not happy at this point. One after one, the guys got rigged up and stumbled their way to the edge with a guide under each arm to take their weight and the rope; they jumped no problem. I don't remember much from that point until the last guy jumped. He jumped as if he had been doing this all his life. I looked down as he freefell into the gorge and down towards the river at the bottom. He was violently jolted about once the slack was taken up and rope pulled tight. It frightened me. I was not happy, and I was next and last to go. I think I had psyched myself out by watching the guys. I was pacing up and down the underside of the bridge stressing out. The guides clearly see this all the time. I really did not want to do this. I didn't trust the whole thing. I didn't like the look of the ropes and felt completely out of control. I had no way of controlling this in any way, and it stressed me out. They called me over and began to hook me up, and I was surprised how basic the whole set up was. Once I did the jump they had a guy hanging under the bridge that was going to turn me around and winch me back up to the spot I jumped from.

I was sat on a plastic seat with two guys checking I was strapped up properly, and then I stood up. One of them went under each arm and helped me across to the jump spot. One of them took the weight of the rope and told me to just stand strong and look at the horizon; don't look down. He gently dropped the weight of the bungie cord over the bridge and let it hang clear. The weight of it hanging there shocked me; it felt like I was going to get pulled off by it. I said "No, No!" I'm not going, and they moved me back from the edge. That feeling of fear running through my veins and my mind going wild was in control. I was terrified. I couldn't think straight; all I could see in my head was the guy before me getting whanged around down there at the end of the rope.

I said I wanted to try again. In hindsight; I now realise this was not a fully committed attempt. I didn't really want this, and I was going to try again, but I wasn't going at it with all my heart. They went through the same process again getting me over to the edge, slipping the rope off the edge, and holding me there with one of them under each arm. Once again, I looked to the horizon, but my gaze kept being broken by the urge to look down. They started to count me in. "One ... two ..."

"No, f£$k!" I grabbed both of them with some sort of newly found strength and lifted them enough to be able to get back a step from the edge. I'd had enough; I wasn't doing this. I wasn't here out of choice – I was scared as f£$k and felt completely out of control. I was the 11th person in the world not to do the jump!

In hindsight, I have no regrets about it at all. I would be more annoyed if it was something I really wanted to do. I was overcome by fear. I was 18 years old at the time, and it was probably one of the first times I remember being really scared to the point of not doing something. I think now I would possibly be able to do it. I still don't want to do it; it's not of interest to me, but if my life depended on it, I would find a way I imagine.

11

DRUNK SCUMBAG

This is a situation I found myself in with Sara, yet I didn't feel fear or anxiety and certainly not panic, neither did she, but I saw how fear overwhelmed someone else during it, and they began to panic. So, Sara and I had decided to have dinner behind the harbour wall on the north side of the harbour at sunset. We had takeaway pizzas and were sitting by the sea to eat them. It was a beautiful summer's evening, and the town was busy, so we hid down by the sea behind the wall for a couple of hours' peace and quiet while the rest of the town was overrun with tourists. We had parked up near Barry's Amusements, and once we finished dinner after the sun had set we began to walk back to the van. We were coming along the quayside when I noticed someone standing on the harbour bridge shouting at someone in the water. My first reaction is normally to run and try to help, but I quickly realised this guy was drunk, and other people were shouting at them both. They were being loud and disturbing the peace in the area. I could see other people were intimidated by them and were looking sheepish. To be completely honest, I think I made a mistake at this point getting too close. The guy was leaning on the left-hand side of the bridge handrail shouting down at his mate in the water. He had his back to the footpath on the bridge, so I figured we could slip behind him unnoticed and not draw any attention. I moved to keep Sara on the safer side away from him, and we entered the end of the bridge; we got closer, and he continued shouting at his mate, and I thought we got away with it before I heard him walking behind us. I knew he had no bottles or weapons in his hands, so I wasn't scared of that, and I assumed he might walk up behind us and then disappear back to his mate. He didn't. He went up behind Sara as we continued to walk through a crowded area on the other side of the bridge, and without touching her, he walked close making noises right behind her head. Other people were looking in our direction. Neither of us flinched, we just sped up our walking and didn't look directly back at him. I didn't for one second feel any fear or emotion – I was simply waiting for my opportunity to deal with him. Bang! I spun around and hit him full whack with the heels of both hands on his chest to create space, and he went flying backwards. He went from drunk gobby lout to apologetic submissive drunk gobshite pleading with me not to hit him. He was like a 45-year-old human deer in the headlights, wide-eyed, praying I was not going to bury him in the ground. I had no intention of escalating it unless he tried to; what I had done was ample given the situation and how he was behaving. I was never scared in this instance, but he went from cocky, arrogant, and full of himself to petrified in a split second. He didn't envisage for one second that I was going to use the element of surprise against him. He was in shock, and he was now fearful of what was coming next. I could see all this dawn on him in an instant, and he immediately apologised as he backed up and stumbled backwards away from us. We didn't move from our spot, and he disappeared out of sight, and we turned and continued our walk back to the van. He was overcome by fear and unable to function properly. He was jabbering and panicking as he tried to speak and was clearly wondering what was coming next. He had no time to prepare for that immediate fear coming over him, so he started to flap. Had I not had the opportunity and used the element of surprise, I may not have disarmed him suddenly enough to put the fear of God in him, and it may have escalated quickly. I used fear and a sudden shock rather than extreme violence to keep him at bay, and luckily it worked. It's interesting how some dickhead, apparently drunk, sobers up very quickly when he has too!

12

PILLION

I am riding my pushbike along the coast road from Portrush to 'The Pits', close to Portstewart. The odd car whizzes past me, but the roads are closed to the public. I'm on my way to The North West 200, a famous motorcycle road race. I'm not going to spectate – I'm going to take part, well kind of. A week prior to this, I had taken one of the most successful racers out surfing. We were filming a program for the BBC in which I introduced Michael Dunlop to big wave surfing, and he introduced me to road racing. Michael comes from undoubtedly the most successful of road racing families in history. All his family have done things most human beings can only imagine. We spoke about the similarities in big wave surfing and motor cycle racing. Both require us to be willing to go to places in our minds most people don't want to. 99.9999% of people will only ever be onlookers, observers of what we do. A very few people ever become motorcycle road racers, and very few people ever become big wave surfers. Both take a lifelong obsession, lifelong commitment, lifelong dedication, and lifelong sacrifice. In some instances, the sacrifice is life itself. Yet, we still do it. We know the risks. Each sport has its dangers, some may be considered worse in some ways than others depending on where you are looking at them from. Ultimately, anything that has the potential to cause serious harm or potentially kill a person breeds fear. That's why the numbers of people involved stay very low, outbalanced by the number of intrigued onlookers, spectators, and fans of the hell men charging onwards. Few people have the desire, the will, the ability to surf big waves, and road race motorcycles. Those individuals that rise to the challenge are masters in the management of fear and know intimately how they react and perform in intricate detail at the very limits of what is deemed possible.

The plan was that between two races, Michael was going to take me for a lap of the track on a superbike. My mind approached this like it was a huge swell on the forecast. I didn't sleep properly for two days in advance. I tossed and turned at night thinking and worrying about all sorts of things. I even tried to imagine if we had an accident at high speed what I was going to do if I had any chance to react during it. Upon arrival at the Riders Village in The Pits, motorcycle legend Phillip McCallen took me to try and get leathers to fit me. He took me to the Suzuki truck to get leathers from "The Two Metre Man". This guy might have been the same height as me, but he was about five stone lighter. I tried to get the leathers on, and they got as far as my calves! Surfing all my life has resulted in huge calves. These weren't going to work. Then we went off to meet "Big Mac", another big guy who was more my size but quite a bit shorter. I got into his leathers even though they were like pedal pushers on me. There I was waddling around the pits with pedal pusher leathers on and a saggy arse. I wear a skin-tight neoprene wetsuit every day with no issues whatsoever, but right then I felt like a complete idiot. I stood with Michael and Phillip for a moment, and we discussed what was going to happen, and the BBC rigged up the cameras and microphones. I have to say I knew nothing of motorbikes until this. I stood and looked at the bike we were going to go on. It was clearly not built for two riders, just one, and certainly not two big lads. I was wondering how this was really going to work, but Michael didn't seem bothered. He started to walk the bike to the start line. I was feeling scared at this point. Michael sat forward and let me step over and on behind him. He said when we were braking hard, push to push my weight off him using the petrol tank so I didn't push him forward and off the handlebars, and just hold on tight, and if he went too quickly just to give him a squeeze. I replied with, "No, I won't be squeezing, you just do what you do. I'm here for the ride ... let's go!" He started to pull away, and I was terrified. I literally couldn't look. I tucked my head down behind him, so I didn't see what was going on. Then I realised the bike felt so strong and solid the quicker we went, and I felt much better. I envisaged it being unstable, but it seemed to be that the faster it went, the forces kept it steadier on the road. Within about 100 yards and going into the first corner, I looked up and over his shoulder and we were already at 75 mph. This was amazing! Most of the fear left me at this point, and I went into the zone. It was just like being out in big surf, feeling the fear in advance to the point of being consumed by it to it then totally disappearing in the moment of complete focus. We flew through corner after corner into the sharp left at Station Road and then took off up the road towards the roundabout. It was from here that it became something else. We took off down past Trolans', and as we came into the bend at the railway crossing, we were about an inch from the kerb at 140 mph. It was amazing! We hit 170 mph on that straight down to the university corner. We leaned into the corner, and then all off a sudden the bike came up onto one wheel as he blipped it on the incline. For a second or two we were wheelieing up the hill. Fear immediately came back, and I gripped on tight thinking, *oh shit, here we go. I'm about to come off the back of this thing.* The tyre regripped the road, and we tore on up and around the roundabout where it happened again as he started to power his way out and onto the Portrush road. I thought, *f£$k me I'm coming off now*, but again the bike torqued itself straight as he kept the speed on, and we took off down the straight. I was really interested to see how he would drive as he approached the bend that his father had been killed the year before. I expected him to ease up a little, but in true warrior fashion, if anything, he went faster. This man is a machine, a weapon. We hit 165 mph as we passed the Hillcrest then into Church corner. The edges of the black stone railway tunnel just inches from us as we sped into the notorious black hill stretch that has seen so many accidents over the years. We crossed the finish line, and as we pulled up, the BBC cameras were straight in my face. Speechless, I didn't know where to begin. What a rush that was. I put total faith and trust in an elite expert, and he didn't hold back.

Even though he had me on board, he totally committed. It was just like the turmoil I go through in advance of big swells and then the deathly calm I enter in the moment.

So many people called me, "f£$kin mental, of all the people to go on the back of, you went with a Dunlop; they are the craziest of the lot."

You see, I beg to differ. These men are not crazy; they are highly skilled and highly comfortable in places in the mind and in situations most people cannot fathom. They have continually been scared throughout life, but they kept going to the point they are now comfortable at 200 mph on a road bike! That's the same as big wave surfers. It starts at one ft., and it keeps going! Fears are faced on an ongoing basis, the fear threshold continually pushed, and suddenly what is normal to most people driving at 45 mph or surfing two-foot waves becomes comfortable for road racers in excess of 170 mph and for big wave surfers above 30 feet. The willingness to expose ourselves to the fear repeatedly is just part of the journey in our chosen field. It is not something we even spend much time thinking about; we just keep going to the best of our abilities.

This was one of the best experiences of my life!

13

THE F£$KING DENTIST

People are often surprised to hear that although I do all these things at sea in big waves, and I feel anxious long before doing them but rarely fear for my life, I do really fear the dentist. I have always hated the dentist. I particularly hate anything to do with teeth. My fear was so bad I didn't go to the dentist for 11 years! I even managed to avoid the dentist for another six years with a hole in my tooth which was sore if I ate on that side of my mouth. If that doesn't describe pure fear and total avoidance of the situation, I don't know what would.

I have always had good strong teeth; I didn't have any fillings until I was 26, and even now I only have a couple. I can remember one specifically traumatic experience that made me fear the dentist. When I was a kid, they put the brackets on my teeth to attach braces to. I hated it so much I demanded they were taken off within the first week of having them. Obviously, all involved were very persistent in their attempts to persuade me to keep them on, but I was completely sure I'd rather have a couple of wonky teeth than have those things in my mouth. They were removed, but the dentist was not impressed with me!

So, 11 years later, I decided it was time to face this. I needed to check I wasn't doing myself harm not getting checked up, so I thought I would go along. Considering I wasn't in any pain or whatever, I figured they would probably give me a quick check over, and that would be that. Well, I was wrong! Literally the worst thing that could happen happened!

I really hate the front teeth, anything touching them makes me squirm. He decided to clean up around the gum line with that wee drill thing! Oh boke! I lay on the chair with half my legs hanging off the end because I'm so tall clinging onto the arms of the chair for dear life whilst the dentist used that thing around my mouth. It was horrific! I literally just wanted to get out of the chair, but I stared at the ceiling and pretended I was surfing! I envisaged myself in extreme detail being in the water, paddling for a wave and surfing. I watched the wave break around me, and I was as close to being there as I ever could be without being there. The sound of the drill disappeared, and I was in a wee world of my own for a while until he stopped and made me spit the blood out!

I honestly couldn't believe I had to go through that; I didn't even know that was a thing they did! It didn't stop there. I needed a filling! I was like, *oh no*! He explained he was going to have to inject me to numb the area and that would take around ten minutes to kick in before he could work on me, and in that time,

I could sit out in the waiting area while he looked at someone else. I thought, *oh, Jesus Christ not a needle in my upper gums no, please*! Of course, it was a top tooth, and he had to inject around its gum. Again, I lay down in the chair and stared at the ceiling. The arms of the chair were again under extreme pressure as I gripped them, and I was back surfing at a great point break. Once he had finished, I went out to the waiting area. I sat down in silence beside a man and a woman. The man was reading some leaflet, and the woman was just sitting there staring into space and thinking. I was in shock; I'd just come thinking I would get away with a wee checkup ... *The f£$ker stuck that drill thing up under my gums, now he has injected me with some shite, and I'm about to go back in for another prodding!* The woman asked me what I was getting done, and as I went to reply, I realised I now had a rubber gub, and it felt like my tongue was hanging out of my mouth. Now I felt stupid. She smirked as I tried to speak. Then she was called into the dentist in the other room, and I stuck my finger in my mouth to discover I couldn't feel it! I sat there for ten minutes hoping that the man wasn't going to look up and break into conversation. I quickly grabbed a magazine and pretended to read it intently. It was some women's magazine, so I figured hopefully the fact I was engrossed in a women's magazine might be enough to make him think I'm some weirdo!

The dentist calls me back in, here we go! Now I'm f£$king shitting myself. I sit back down in the seat, and he sticks his rubber covered finger in my mouth and has a good feel around. Within seconds, I hear a drill starting, and I'm like, *oh my f£$kin God*! He notices I'm shitting myself and tries to reassure me. He sticks the drill into my tooth, and I'm flinching and jolting every time he moves. Turns out my mouth wasn't frozen enough! *F£$k me; first the cleaning of the gum line then the injections, and now I'm being poked in the raw nerve by a drill*! *Wtf*! He then brings out the needle again and begins to ram some more of that into me! He says you are a big lad, maybe I didn't have the dose right the first time. He pokes me like I'm a pin cushion and sends me back out to the waiting room. Now I feel like an idiot. Not only is my gum going numb, the right-hand side of my tongue is too and my lip! I feel like I must look severely swollen and deformed, and I try to hide in the magazine again until he calls me back in. This time he sits me down. I can't feel a bloody thing, and he starts with the drill again! He eventually fills the tooth as I sit there in the chair clinging onto the arms with sweat running down my face!

I had totally faced my fear, and I was caught with things happening I couldn't have dealt with or prepared for other than just rolling with it. It was horrific, but I figured it was most likely not going to ever be as bad as that again, and so I went for checkups every year after that. I have since endured a couple of fillings and once the removal of a tooth. It was the worst. He didn't want to remove it so tried to fill it and support it that way, but when I phoned him to tell him the entire right-hand side of my head and neck were in agony, he told me to get in there asap; it must come out. So, in true me fashion, he couldn't get it out! My jaw and teeth are obviously big and strong, and he was basically on top of me trying to wrench this thing out of my head! He was having so much difficulty getting the tooth out that after ten minutes he decided to have a wee break for a rest and sent me out to the waiting room with the tooth still in my head, only this time half of it had been broken off, and the other half was hanging loose! It was horrific! I couldn't believe what was happening to me. I hate dentists, and once again, I'm going through something which is far from textbook; nothing is ever easy or straight forward with me! He eventually got it out, and then I had to endure stitching the gum! Honestly, I didn't know any of these things happened in a dentist's, and I have never heard stories like them from anyone else but me!

14

UNCHARTED WATERS – FEAR OF THE UNKNOWN

Have you ever heard the phrase uncharted waters? That comes from the sea, obviously. If you look at ocean charts that have been surveyed to show mariners' depths, hazards, way points, currents, etc., to plot a course you would be mistaken to think that they are 100% accurate. Some of the information is not accurate because it is often impossible to survey parts of the sea and coast for various reasons such as depth. For that reason, some areas are not charted either correctly or at all, and it's simply local knowledge   that   provides   people   with   the information to navigate the waters. I have first-hand experience of this.

My favorite thing over the years has been to search for new big wave surf spots. This means spots that haven't been discovered and haven't been ridden. I've spent a lot of time doing this, and I've discovered and ridden a lot of locations off the beaten track so to speak. In 2003, I began a project that I called *'Project Red'* in which I used a boat and ocean charts to search the waters from as far east as Rathlin Island in The North Channel between Scotland and Northern Ireland and as far to the south west as Sligo Bay in the Republic of Ireland. If there is an outcrop of rock, a sea mount, a submerged ledge where waves break off that entire coastline, I visited it, ruled it in as a possible big wave spot or ruled it out. I have a hoard of battered ocean charts scribbled all over with notes on lots of areas. The spots that had surf-able waves I returned to time and time again and surfed, some more than others. Even today, 15 years later, I am still getting to know these spots, their ideal conditions, their personalities, their potential, their dangers. These spots are often uncharted and escape survey by organisations due to them being shallow or continually covered with surf. So, think about this for a minute. If I wanted to go surfing at the local beach, it's straight forward, sand, beach, possibly a rip current, and waves. If I want to go surfing somewhere far off the coast that hasn't even been surveyed properly or at all, I really do not know anything about the location except what I can see with my eyes at the time. I do not know if there is a wreck on the sea bed; is there an underwater cave I may get stuck in if I fall on a big wave? Is there rock extremely close to the surface? I have surfed waves where the charts told me it was five metres deep only to discover I could stand in waist deep water out there! Clearly, no one had ever been on the reef to really check it out, so someone made an estimate and wrote it on the chart. All these factors are unknowns, and they make my attempt to ride huge waves more difficult and exciting. One thing I know is that I don't have any information to go on. I know no one has done this before – they haven't hit the bottom while trying to surf a big wave – they haven't experienced the currents, etc., and I don't know if there is anything underwater that I should be particularly concerned about. All these unknowns create a very different level of fear compared to what I might experience at my local beach, for example, where I have surfed for 30 years, and so have several other people in all sorts of conditions and sizes of waves. I vividly remember one day at a spot I call 'Voices', an isolated, submerged rock ledge off the coast which I had been surfing for a couple of winters before I had a frightening experience where I got smashed by a really big, violent wave. I was OK, but I was underwater wondering what may be down there as this wave took aim and unloaded right onto me hitting me with immense power. It wasn't until a session there years later, on an unusually low tide that I saw this huge nobble of rock sticking out through the face of the wave! I didn't know that was there! A couple of local fisherman in the area warned me on different occasions about the rock coming out of the surface, but despite surfing there on all tides and various conditions, I never saw it until this one day the tide was really low, and the surf conditions aligned. Huge evil black peat-stained barrels were detonating onto the barely covered reef, and three of us were catching waves. My friend Tim even got murdered by a big set wave, but the rock didn't show its face until a couple of hours later when the tide went dead low and the waves got even bigger. These unknown factors make the whole thing much scarier, make me think of all the worst-case scenarios, and may stop me ever riding a wave at certain locations. How can I deal with some of those fears? I can snorkel, or scuba dive the reef on a calm day, see exactly what's down there. I can visit the location in a range of different conditions and get to know it and how the water behaves in certain conditions, etc. I basically build up as much information as I can in advance of riding a wave. I try to make the unknown less important to the situation so that I can eventually focus on riding the huge waves that may break there and the fear that that brings. I try to control everything I can long in advance of surfing a wave there.

The same principle can be applied to any fear related to the unknown. Yes, we may not be able to completely eradicate the unknown, but we can educate ourselves in as many ways as possible to lessen its effect upon us. I have no idea what a big wave may do as I am riding it; I can't control that, it's an unknown quantity, a wild animal, that I am only able to deal with during the ride, and to be quite honest, that is a huge part of my attraction to surfing. Experience from surfing allows me to adjust in a split second as I ride a wave to stay on my board and not fall off.

However, all the other things that worry me are things I can deal with by spending a bit of time considering them and gaining knowledge of them, therefore lessening their psychological effect on me and allowing me to reach my goal of surfing huge waves at that location. I could easily say, "You know what, as big and inviting as these waves are and as much as I want to surf them, there are too many things that I don't know the answer to, so it's better I don't try to surf here." It's different if it's too dangerous because there is something very specific that would tip the risk balance against me, but if it's just the unknown quantities in my way that are scaring me such as what's on the reef – is there a wreck, is there an underwater cave, etc.? – then it would be bad for me not to deal with those and lessen the impact caused by the fear of not knowing. If I said, "F£$k it, I'm doing it anyway," it would be irresponsible and reckless. I have responsibilities in life far beyond catching a few big waves, and throwing caution completely to the wind is unfair on many people in my life.

In my experience, almost all fear hinges on the unknown; the less I know, the more there is to worry about. Some may say, the more known, the more there is to worry about, but I don't agree with that. Knowing, removes the unknown, it narrows things down and clears unnecessary doubt and wonder from the mind allowing space to focus on performance, enjoying the moment, and creating memories. The more I can learn ahead of being in whatever the situation, surf spot, room, environment, group, etc., the less there is to worry about, the less there is that can creep up and catch me off guard and cause me to panic when I should be focusing on something else. It could be I should be focusing on surfing and not all the potential things that could happen along the way; it could be something in everyday life. Fear isn't just isolated to extreme danger and craziness, it's obviously in all different walks of life and in all different situations, but the same principle in my opinion is true whether it be a potentially life-threatening situation or something much less so.   Fear hinges on the unknown; control how many unknown factors effect what it is I am attempting to do, and I control the amount of fear likely to be present, and I massively reduce the risk of panic ever setting in.

15

HELL AND HIGH WATER

It was a winter Tuesday afternoon, and my team at the time which consisted of two brothers, Howard and Richard, and photographer Charles, were tracking a big wild storm as it moved up the Atlantic heading towards us. Ricky wasn't going to be available for what looked like the arrival of the peak of the swell on Thursday morning. We needed Ricky to pilot our little RIB (Rigid Inflatable Boat) named Beard Commander (BC). Ricky is a world champion natural bodybuilder and had hurt his elbows in training at the weekend. Howard and I were going to be the tow team with Charles shooting pictures, but we needed a backup driver for the boat. In lots of situations, I will not go to sea if I don't have the right team around me. This swell looked to be huge, and so I was trying to work out how we were going to do it. I phoned my mate, Hanno, a German guy that moved to Northern Ireland a few years ago. It turned out his family had a yacht with a small tender boat when he was a kid, so he knew how to drive on flat water, so I reckoned I could bring him up to speed quickly. He agreed to a quick training session on Wednesday afternoon at Portballintrae and then to come with us on Thursday morning.

Hanno arrived at the slipway on Wednesday as I hauled the boat out of my van and into the water. It was a dark stormy day; the swell was already smashing the north coast. The little bay at Portballintrae next to the harbour had huge lines of whitewater pushing all the way to shore and surging up the beach. It was raging. The wee boat is nippy, but I was kind of scared we might flip it in these conditions, but at the same time, I knew that tomorrow might be even worse, and if Hanno couldn't handle it here, then he wouldn't be up for the job tomorrow.

We lifted the little 15hp engine onto the transom of the boat, pull started it, and she coughed into life. I gave Hanno a quick run through of operating it and gave him the tiller, and away we went. As we left the slip and the safety of the pier, he had to time it to nip in between one whitewater surge and the next one. Hanno took the boat out into the deeper water in the middle of the bay and quickly got the hang of maneuvering it and using the throttle. There was a huge set breaking out at the mouth of the bay. It was rumbling and surging towards us. 20 feet of whitewater was across the bay heading for shore with us in this wee rubber boat ready to be swept up by it. Hanno started to get the boat planing, but we were side on to this wall of whitewater. I was shouting, "Turn the f£$kin boat let's go!" We were rushed by the whitewater as Hanno swung the boat towards shore at the last minute. Thankfully, the wave backed off enough that the engine propeller didn't cavitate, and we didn't get swamped and sunk

... just soaked. We outran the wave until it backed off just before shore and reformed into a breaking wave. Back out we went again to toy with it a bit more! We spent half an hour before dark in pissing rain and wild ocean surges pushing the wee boat and Hanno to the max until we were happy to get back on land and prepare for the dawn mission and the peak of the swell. We had a full team! I phoned Howard and told him the good news; we were good to go, and he planned to be ready to roll at 4 a.m.

Going to bed at midnight and setting the alarm for 3 a.m. seems like a pointless exercise knowing full well that those three hours may result in about an hour of sleep, an hour of tossing and turning, and an hour of fretting about something I forgot to pack but have told myself I will do when I get up. I was worried about Hanno; this was going to be his first time in the team, and we were going far off the coast in huge seas. I know he was excited and probably a little in the dark as to what to expect in the morning. I lost a lot of sleep over it that night, but I reckoned Howard and I could handle whatever came our way, and the other guys would be OK. It's very easy to just say No at times, but gut feeling counts for a lot in my experience when it comes to being unsure, anxious, and scared. Deep down seems to overrule the head's uncertainties I find. I normally only go out on big days with a team that have trained together and who know each other and what to expect in each other. However, on this occasion we were somewhat rolling the dice, but there remained the feeling that we would pull together.

The place we were going was far offshore where a rise in the seabed from 50m to 0m forces deep open ocean swells to stand up abruptly as they run into this considerable shipping hazard causing them to break with extreme power and energy. It is extremely raw out there. The sea is unruly; it is often plagued by bad wind, and there is a current running across the reef making the dark peat-stained waves warp and wobble as they hit the reef. My friend at the local University is an Oceanographer that helps me study the seabed and local waters off all these spots I find. He has worked with me since 2003 and supplies me with data, charts, 3D models, etc. of the spots. It helps that he has dived on some of them too. He led a student dive trip to this location at a time. So, I have a lot of expert knowledge to hand from him when I need it. There are some other more exposed locations than this, but this one is particularly wild. I call this wave Area 70 as it sits close to a bleak outcrop which is known as Eire 70. The next headland is known as Eire 71. The two of them historically mark the flight corridor for the allied planes during the war showing them the safest route to fly up into Barnesmore Gap to the north. This is a spot I have seen for a long time far out at sea, and it turns out that the first day I surfed there was the biggest and cleanest I've surfed it to date. Huge clean 50-foot waves breaking consistently far out at sea when the spots on the coast were only 10 feet! On that day, I led a four-man crew out there, and I was the only one that wanted to surf. I honestly thought I would be riding very big clean waves there a lot, but its exposure to the elements has meant that the first day happens to have been the best. Nearly every session since has not been as expected except one big glassy paddle day on a day with no wind and bright sunshine. So, as I lay in bed, I was not expecting beautiful conditions; I was expecting harsh wild end of the earth type stuff, and although Howard, Charles, and I had experienced that several times before out there, the inclusion of new blood was making me nervous. It could be argued I was overthinking it, but I'm always so aware of people not realising what they are getting themselves into when they come to play with me! It's so important that everyone comes home after the day, and I know that it takes real experience at times to handle crazy situations that are never too far away in the world of riding big waves of the wild Irish coast.

I got up, feeling confident and full of energy despite virtually no sleep. I walked outside my house to see a taxi sitting halfway up the street with its engine running. It must have just dropped off people who had been out for the night; it was early Sunday morning, after all. The sky was full of stars and not a breath of wind. Another taxi swung into the street as I began to load the last few things into the van, the driver looking at me out the window with, "Where on earth is he going surfing at this time?" I was concerned that the low-pressure system that was due to be centering over Area 70 in the night giving it calm conditions had, in fact, centered over Portrush instead. This would mean potentially windy conditions at the break. I checked the wave buoys moored at approximately 50 miles and 200 miles offshore, and they were still reading a solid six metres, so in theory, there would be huge waves regardless of wind. I pushed my new board into the van over the top of the boat and gently shut the doors so as not to wake the neighbours. I hooked on the jet ski trailer to the tow hitch and went back indoors. I have got into a habit recently of making a cup of tea before leaving for a mission; it seems to make me stop for a few minutes and calm the jitters. I had a few minutes left before I had to go pick the guys up, so I put the kettle on and chilled before creeping out of the street. The first port of call for me was to collect Hanno at his house. He lives just down the road from me, and I was to meet him at

0350. As I approached his house, he was standing in the dark on the footpath with all his gear beside him, eating a bowl of porridge. We loaded his gear into the van then set off to collect Charles and Howard before heading down the icy road to the west coast.

The closer we got to the west coast, the more the ice became water, and the heavier it began to rain. The clear skies became heavy and overcast, much more like what I'm used to seeing on these big wave missions. There was a real sense of gloom in the air with low lying thick cloud and relentless rain on the windshield. I became increasingly concerned about the wind at Area 70. The harbour is tucked into a little corner where steep green fields meet the sea. A one-track lane leads down to it. It's rarely used except in summer, and when the tide is low, the slipway hangs high and dry out of the water. One time as we pulled in here with a slightly different crew, we witnessed the ghostly sight of three Catholic nuns standing on the quayside dressed in full habit. Eerily they stood motionless and staring at the sea into which we were headed! One of them was even taking pictures of the wild sea in the distance. Initially, we all said, "What the f£$k!" Then there was silence. It was a creepy sight. Once we pulled up and parked, they didn't speak to us; they continued standing there for a few minutes before all squeezing into a little granny mobile and disappearing up the lane! Weird!

Conditions at the harbour were good. There wasn't a breath of wind, and we saw smoke from a chimney rising vertically into the air just around the corner. However, there was a slight chop on the water surface which led me to believe that it must be windier at sea. It's funny; it doesn't matter how perfect conditions are or how great things are in general, I never fully settle until I am out there and can see and feel what's going on. Beforehand, I am continually checking weather charts, wave buoys, etc. and wondering, worrying, second guessing. I never settle down – I'm full of what ifs. What then and the like. It's as if I know no matter how prepared we are, we are never prepared enough.

There are huge unknown factors in every big wave session let alone at locations far out at sea at places no one has ever surfed before. We decided to get ready anyway and get out there. Quite often, I feel really drained upon arrival at a slipway or a beach because I've spent the previous two days buzzing around getting ready and making plans before even surfing, but this morning I was upbeat and ready to go! We were almost completely set up as the morning light began to show.

We got all our gear on. I didn't feel fear of the waves that morning – I felt fear of the conditions. I knew we were in a tiny little protected corner, and I was fearful of what we were going to face as we rounded the headland to the south and faced the storm head-on. I always find myself taking involuntary deep breaths and exhales when I feel this anxiety.

The tide was almost over-spilling onto the remote harbour wall. It was due to drop by 4.4m, so we knew it would disappear quickly. We launched the wee boat first. It is 3.4m long with a rigid hull and Hypalon tubes. It fits perfectly into my van, so we don't need to trailer another vessel across country. Hanno climbed aboard and warmed the engine up around the harbour for ten minutes while Howard and I slipped the ski in. My new 14'2" board has an extra leash plug built into it at a specific spot so that it can be tied to the rescue sled and transported more easily. Tying big boards onto the ski or sled is always an issue. Howard and I tied it on, and we passed Hanno and Charles, who was now aboard the boat, my tow board to keep for the ride out. By the way, I think it is important to note at this point Charles can't swim, not a bit, just floats there, bobs about, gets dragged about by one of us and has a heart condition. Yes, that's right, and he is now sat up in the bow of the beard commander with Hanno at the helm who only yesterday had his first run in the boat! Hence, my nervousness and uncertainty in the current forecast.

I'm pretty stubborn when I have something in mind, and in the past, I would only bring a big wave gun out so that I would be forced to paddle and not tow, but I've had a few shockers lately taking that approach in bad conditions which would have been better suited to towing. So lately, especially at Area 70, I've been bringing both tow gear and paddle gear.

The last time we went out to Area 70, we got hit with really bad conditions. All the guys were sick. It was so rough out there. It rattled Charles a little and literally left him severely bruised down one side of his body from the pounding he was getting aboard the boat in the choppy seas and verging on hypothermia. This time, he asked if it would ever be as bad as that again, and I said no, but I kind of lied. The forecast for today was supposed to be one of the days where the wind goes completely still for a few hours because the centre of the low pressure was due to pass over us. The forecast had been changing by the hour for the past five days, so I knew it was going to be either perfect conditions or most likely wild conditions as the strongest winds in a low-pressure system spin around the edge of the centre. So literally, a 50-mile movement of the low-pressure system's location could make or break our session.

The tide was dropping fast; we fired up the ski and headed out into the open ocean clear of the headlands.

As expected, the low had moved and not in our favour. We were now head-on into choppy grey rough seas with a big swell running and a strong head wind. I knew this was going to be hard on us all. The last day this happened, the swell was slightly bigger, but it looked to me like we were going to encounter harsher conditions, so I was worried about Charles. This guy has a heart condition and can't swim! Not only did he have to have heart surgery, but he rigged the operating theatre with cameras that he could operate during the operation using a remote trigger. He knows no limits, and as the saying goes: he suffers for his art but does it without even thinking about it, it's just who he is. The last day we came out here, it took us 40 minutes to get out to the spot.

Today, I could see the wave breaking from a long way off in the distance, and it looked ridiculously big, but I knew the swell was due to drop quickly with the dropping tide, so we needed to get on it quickly. Hanno was piloting the boat, and Howard was at the helm of the ski with me on behind him. Howard and I were leading the way to break the chop for Hanno and Charles, so they sat in behind us on the boat and got a bit of shelter. At one stage when I looked back at them, they were far down in the trough of a huge open ocean swell as Howard and I motored up over the top. They looked so tiny, insignificant, and vulnerable in the vast greyness. Streaks of white bled through the surface of the water as the wind howled across it. The tiny little boat containing two men continually disappeared in chop and mountainous swell passing by.

Howard dropped back to check on them once we were about halfway out as it was taking us a long time to make headway in the chop. As they pulled up alongside, Hanno looked like the conditions weren't bothering him in the slightest and sat there with a big smile on his face wrapped up in his 6mm suit, huge coat, and hiking boots. He looked pretty at home! Charles on the other hand was suffering badly. He was already extremely cold, so we stopped and went through everything to warm him up. I had originally tried to distract him by trying to make a joke of it and get him laughing with general abuse and talking and stuff, but he was having none of it. I tried slagging him a bit but still nothing; he wasn't impressed! All of us are trained and experienced in giving first aid and lots of other things at sea so we all recognised straight away that he was showing signs of hypothermia. All his movements were slow, and he was beginning to hunch over. His hands and feet were frozen, but he said his body wasn't, yet he was shivering so much, his jaw was rattling. The boat was taking on a lot of water, and he was struggling to keep bailing as Hanno piloted. He was lying in about eight inches of water curled up with his head under the red spray deck at the bow next to the fuel tank. Hanno had flasks of hot water in the boat for exactly this scenario, so he got them out and began pouring them onto Charles' feet and hands. Charles was struggling to put the lid back on the flask and was, in fact, turning it the wrong way, which I took as a sign of hypothermia, not thinking straight. He was starting to lose it. He demanded that we kept going and that we weren't giving up, but Howard and I had other plans. We agreed with him, but we both said to ourselves that he had five minutes left, and if he hadn't improved, then we are aborting.

The period we spent stopped lost us 15 minutes of travel time as we drifted back towards where we came from in the wind. We were only halfway there, and already 40 minutes had gone. We led them out another five minutes before checking again, and somehow Charles had improved. He had hunkered down in the bow of the boat and had begun to warm up. We kept going. One thing that made me laugh was taking a quick glimpse into the boat, and in the eight inches of water swilling around, Hanno had resorted to wrapping two plastic bags from the supermarket Lidl over his feet and tied them above his ankles. It was comedy in a dark moment! Charles curled up in the bow wearing all his clothes over his wetsuit and my ski jacket and Howard's hi vis jacket over that, and Hanno sitting there wearing his shopping bags with a massive grin on his face!

We stopped a couple more times to check on Charles, but he had improved slightly and was determined that we should keep going. The weather was so bad and the cloud so low it caused us to lose sight of all landmarks at times. Both Howard and I knew we were already pushing the limits at this stage so far out at sea, and if anything happened, we were going to be in the shit big style. We spotted a commercial fishing boat a couple of miles away and agreed that if Charles took a turn for the worse we would make a dash for it to get him dry at least, and if we had no choice, we would call for support from there. I know this sounds completely mental so far, but all of us know that it takes boundaries to be pushed to make things happen sometimes, and Charles was doing just that.

I also knew that this was early days at a new location which had the potential to produce huge waves, but all this was part of the learning experience we all needed so that we were comfortable out there in all sorts of scenarios. I must admit though I felt like pulling the plug a couple of times for Charles' sake, but he wanted us to keep going. It was a total of one hour 20 minutes before we made it to the spot!

Howard drove us over to the admiralty mark. A big 4m marker is moored just off the edge of the rock ledge. It sits there silently day in day out witnessing huge unridden waves and standing strong in the face of anything the ocean throws at it. I always use markers and buoys to tie gear or skis to that we are keeping out with us for back-up or that we aren't using right away. Normally, it is difficult to climb aboard it and tie a rope and boards, etc. to as it gets thrown about in the wind and swell like one of those self-righting toys kids have. It has weed hanging off its underside below the waterline, and it all gets exposed for a few seconds when it whips over one way and then disappears when it flips back the other way. The best way to get on is wait for it to get swung low towards me then grab one of the wee metal lips at the edge and let it pull me up out of the water when it swings another way. Then it's cling on for dear life and try to climb up its slimy side before being catapulted off the opposite side and have to start again. Usually, it takes a couple of goes, but yesterday I didn't even try, it was violently whanging around all over the place. I got close enough not to get hit by it, and as soon as it came anywhere near me, I slung a rope in through a steel loop on its side and swam away. Howard then came over and gave me the 14'2" board to secure to it. There was no way I was planning on paddling into a wave myself out there this day. It was chaos; in fact, I wasn't even sure it was safe to tow surf. It was a cauldron. Waves, swell, chop, wind, visibility, and a huge seal were all making things extremely dangerous. I knew that Charles had pushed the boundary a bit to get us out there, so it was my turn to do the same. As I tied the board onto the rope, the buoy snapped away from me, and the carabiner on the end ripped through my neoprene glove making a huge tear in it. My hand was bright red inside and pure white around the fingers. Howard and I were both silent staring at it waiting for my hand to start gushing blood, but somehow, I got lucky and it didn't break the skin. We secured the board and went to look at the wave from the front. It was chaos. The last time it was similar, but maybe a bit bigger and more consistent, but I tried to paddle that day and got no waves. It wasn't huge today, maybe the odd unruly 35-40-footer coming through. It looked like the tide was full despite dropping. I think there was just so much wind, it was pushing a strong current of water over the reef and the waves were being affected by it badly, but the odd one broke with immense force and power, so we knew we had a chance at getting me onto a wild bomb.

Hanno and Charles sat where I suggested was safest to sit just off the edge of the reef, but they were under no illusion that anywhere was safe to sit. Huge side waves wash off the reef out there when the tide is full. The set waves push the water out sideways off the reef, and when it hits the deeper water where I suggested they sit, it gets really chaotic. It's so wild right there that it has thrown me from the jet ski before. But if they were to sit any further away, they couldn't keep an eye on us, and

Charles couldn't shoot the action. Hanno had a skilled job to do on his first day out with us, and he was pulling it off!

Howard and Hanno did a walkie-talkie check and agreed that if either had engine problems or I went down hard what our plan was. That plan was that if I went down hard, then Howard would come get me, the guys in the boat would not get involved unless Howard got cleaned off the ski and we were unable to retrieve it. The guys would then need to make a quick decision as to which of us was in most need and prioritise the rescues ideally before the dry section of the reef came into play further inside the break.

I told Howard I understood it was hard to read the waves out there with such crazy elements but, "Let's just sit and pick a proper big one or at least one that we can see coming from far out that we can line up with." Our normal mark ups on the mountains in the distance were covered by low lying cloud which made it even more intimidating way out there. We went for a couple of waves which didn't really break, and then a bigger one appeared. We didn't have much time, so Howard expertly pulled me up quickly and started charging through the chaos dragging me behind. I was hanging onto the rope trying to keep my board in the water through all the chop and current. Moguls of water were coming up through the wake of the ski trying to throw me off. We were deep on the approach and coming from behind the peak but in front of the approaching swell line. It was a chaotic few seconds. I was shouting at Howard to pick the speed up because I thought I was going to get smashed, but he knew where he was going and positioned me perfectly on the peak and drove up over the shoulder. I remember thinking, *oh shit this is drawing hard* as I let go of the rope and was staring down it building speed. I went airborne over a chop as the massive grey wave detonated into a huge plume of spray in the corner of my left eye. I made the landing and was now going at mach ten straight down the face of this thing winding the windows up (swinging my arms like windmills trying to regain balance without falling backwards into the wave). I hit another ledge and went airborne again, and again I somehow landed it. I was so focused at staying on my board that I ended up straight at the bottom and engulfed in whitewater. I was going so fast, it was mental. I managed to hang on as I got spat out in front of the whitewater and got my board on an edge to try coming around it onto the shoulder, but I got hit again by it and squirted forward again, this time hitting another piece of chop which sent me flying sideways in the air still attached to my board. As I landed on my back, I could see that I was clear of the biggest part of the wave, but the last lip was about to hit me. Boom! I penetrated the surface, got rolled a bit, but nothing too major. I surfaced, the water was chaotic, turbulent, and the next wave was violently rumbling across the reef towards me. Howard was straight in to get me. He was so quick at grabbing me and thankfully so as I could feel the current drag me across the reef towards the impact zone. We went and retrieved my brightly coloured board that had been washed away in the madness. Charles got a couple of shots, and I was like, *right this is seriously pushing the boat out here.*

That wave wasn't anywhere near the biggest wave of my life but was one of the wildest rides I've ever had; in fact, I really don't know how I stayed on – well, in the end, I didn't. We agreed to go on one more and then call it a day. Charles still wanted us to stay out longer and go again, but I know when to stop. I've been doing this long enough to know that boundaries need pushing, but there is a time when we must move on. We packed our stuff onto the skis and boat and began to run with the swell and the wind back towards port.

The next scenario was the boat engine failing. Howard and I wasted no time and threw a rope on the bow and towed them back to harbour. As soon as we docked, I got the engine started on the van, and Charles got in to get changed and warm up. The tide had drained so much that the slipway was now hanging out with no water at the bottom of it. We roped the BC up and dragged it up the slimy slipway. This is always a consideration at this launching spot and has meant waiting a couple of hours before being able to get the ski out. However, Howard needed to be back in Portrush for 16.30, so we didn't have time to wait. There is another slip about 30 minutes away by ski, so he headed back out as I drove the van and trailer to it and waited for him. I normally don't like anyone at sea on one engine alone, but we had radio contact, so if anything happened, we could have got to him quickly. That was one of the most intense missions ever, and I'm sure it will stand us in good stead for all the other sessions we are going to have out there. One thing that hasn't happened yet is me falling on a huge one at that spot. Judging by the power I have felt in the waves every time I have ridden a wave there, I'm expecting that to be as full on as the rest of the experiences at Area 70. With every storm and every swell, I am absorbing more and more information, experience, and knowledge all of which are my weapons against anxiety and fear. I was not worried about the surf this time, more so the conditions and the newly formed team, but we all persevered through some horrific conditions and pulled it off, and we are all better for it. Those experiences together tighten us up, allow us to push hard every time in the knowledge that we have each other, and we will persevere.

16

SNOW PANIC HERE

Hanno was not deterred by his debut experiences in huge seas and decided he wanted to come on board full-time and start to ride some of these waves too. Getting anyone with the desire to face fears and deal with cold and all the madness that comes with chasing huge swells in this part of the Atlantic is not easy to come by. I was really impressed with how he handled the madness at Area 70, and it was good news he wanted more! I started training him on the jet skis next – going through all the different scenarios for rescues, driving at speed and handling the ski in big whitewater. Using jet skis in the surf as a team is so far removed from ordinary surfing that lots of people just don't grasp it and can't be bothered with it, but it's a very useful skill to have in big surf. There are a lot of skills which I believe are easier found in people with a background in the military or police, etc., where they are used to performing in highly stressful situations as if it's a walk in the park. I've had quite a few people in my team from that background over the years. Hanno doesn't have that background, but he brings an air of calmness to the team and seems extremely comfortable in lots of conditions, so we had a head start for training.

Hanno was at the helm of the ski. We had just driven about two miles to the east through dark chaotic storm-driven seas after breaking through huge closeouts across the harbour mouth. The sea was wild, unruly, and menacing, perfect for jet ski work.

We were approaching from offshore towards a westerly facing beach break. The wind was pushing hard behind us and driving snow blizzards onto the shoreline from a black, evil looking horizon. The steep green fields were covered in pure white snow. We had a 20-foot set on our tail, and I was trying to teach Hanno how to handle big walls of whitewater on the ski. I was shouting over the noise of the engine and the weather to tell him we needed to let these slip through and then go on the back of one. The first big unruly swell line came towards us as we rocked sideways in the storm. My feet were freezing, and I was trying to sneak a little shelter behind Hanno whilst peering over his shoulder. Any sudden movement on a day like this, and we end up in the water. The first one passed below us, and we saw the next one starting to approach; he blipped the ski into action, and we motored out and over the big line of unbroken water. As we moved over the top, we were exposed to the blizzard full force. We were approximately three-quarters of a mile offshore at this point, and he banked the ski and started to follow this big one ashore. We were riding on the slope of its back trying to stay close enough but far enough from the one following behind it. The idea was we would turn to face the chasing wave head on once closer to shore and among the chaos.

Hanno began to let the throttle off, and we slowed down and began to create distance between us and the wave in front, making us closer to the next one. "Keep up," I screamed in his ear. He snapped out of it and quickly pulled the throttle to catch up. "Stay close; don't drift off the throttle – we don't have room for error here!" I proclaimed. The wave in front began to break, and the clean, smooth water we were on started to become frothy, then churned up, then became wild whitewater. "Now! bank around and face it head on!" The big dark wave face behind started to turn white, crumble, and roll towards us. We were then trapped between two big broken walls of whitewater. We could outrun to the beach and do various other drills to escape unscathed, but Hanno had done lots of that training, and this training drill was to teach him how to handle big walls of whitewater and to establish what he could and couldn't get away with when under pressure on the ski. It may be that we have an injured surfer on board or in a rush to save someone and there is only one way of getting out of trouble, through the whitewater. So, everyone on the team must be able to handle their ski. "Let's go, bring it around but gently, and once round, DO NOT let the throttle off or it will throw us off the other side!"

"OK," he shouted back. He must turn around and then give us a blip as the wave comes over the bow to propel us up and over it and keep the throttle on to keep us straight. I took a glance over my shoulder, and we were completely surrounded. It was a big wall of turbulent water, and we needed to hit it straight to make it through. He began to turn, and I leaned into it with him. As soon as we completed the 180 degrees move and were facing the whitewater head-on, we capsized. Within a split second, we were both in the water, boards in the water, and the unmanned ski bobbing between us and the incoming wave. We scrambled out of the way and got pummelled by it. I was underwater hoping nothing would hit me with my hands and arms covering my head and curled up in a little ball. We both surfaced, but the ski and boards were gone. Washed ashore in the wave. We began to get hit by wave after wave as we body surfed our way to the shore. We got hold of the ski and dragged its 340kgs up the beach and out of the surf as much as we could on our own. I checked the electrics on the dashboard, and it wasn't working. We had a ski that wouldn't start. We were both roasting after trying to get ashore and pulling the ski out, but I knew we didn't have long before cold set in. It was snowing so hard. The dunes were covered in snow and the beach all the way down to the water mark too. It's not very often we see that on this coast. We needed to move quickly. I made the plan that if we couldn't get the engine started, we would attach a rope and walk and tow it along the shore to the next cove. Then we would swim it with the rope out to sea under the protection of the cliffs to a nearby private harbour and slipway and deal with it from there. I reckoned we had about 90 minutes before pitch black at this point due to so much bad weather coming in.

I pulled the seat off the ski to expose the engine compartment. I didn't really want to let snow in there, but I had no choice. I had a quick look around, and all seemed normal, though I couldn't tell if any water had gone into the air intake which would stop it starting if I had tried to fire it up. I didn't want to have to try and start it when electrics weren't registering, just in case something was soaked. I checked the battery terminals to discover the positive had been shaken loose in the beating the ski got by the wave. We also lost our toolkit in the rolling, meaning we had no way to tighten it up to get the ski to start. I was wearing neoprene gloves, and they are great, but any water sits in the fingers, and in those temperatures, starts to freeze in the wind chill. I had no choice but to take them off; I couldn't work with a battery with wet gloves on. I rolled up my sleeves and pulled the gloves off, exposing me to the snow. The gloves have a wool like lining inside them which repels water and keeps heat in, so I attempted to use it to dry the tips of my fingers enough to have a fiddle at tightening the connection. I tightened the connection as best I could, but it wouldn't bite enough to get the ski to start. I reckoned if I pulled the wires tight and wrapped them around the battery itself then closed the battery support strap, the weight of it might be enough to keep the connection for long enough to get us out of there. I told Hanno to go and hide the boards in the dunes. If this worked, we had to play it safe from there on. We couldn't be trying to punch through big surf on a weak battery connection or we could end up washed ashore again. He came back from hiding the boards, and we dragged the ski down to the edge of the water. The plan was I wrap the wires up and hold them in place as tight as possible. He would start the engine, I throw the seat cover back on, and we drag it into the water and get going. I carefully pulled the wires down the back of the battery, under it, and then back up, and then pull the big rubber support strap over both and fix it in position all whilst trying not to touch the metal connections with wet fingers. It worked; the ski sparked to life, and we dragged it down the water's edge into the surf. I grabbed my gloves from the beach, and we started to travel along the shoreline in shallow water so that if we had a problem, we wouldn't be in immediate danger. Hanno took it slow and easy so as not to cause any sudden jolts to the hull and disrupt our battery connection, going through that a second time might not work. As we reached the far end of the beach, the surf was much smaller due to a protecting headland. We killed time near the shore until there was an opening that would allow us to make a beeline for the private harbour. Once we got there, we would make the call on taking the risk and going back out to sea into the full brunt of the storm to make it to where we launched another mile away. So far so good. We decided to press on. The snow was then sitting in the gunnels and grooves of the ski and on the peak of Hanno's wetsuit hood. We eased our way back out to sea and cut between a shallow rock ledge with large breaking waves and the cliff line. Big surges were rushing off the rocks draining the sea level by three or four metres as the waves washed up and over them then back off before the next one. We were going super slow trying not to get caught by one of those or rushed by whitewater from the waves breaking over the shallow reef to the north. It was a tricky navigational nightmare when we were only doing three knots, but we made it through unscathed. Hanno was taking it easy, and we just cruised our way through the chaotic seas trying not to disturb the battery, on route to the final approach and into the protected harbour and slipway!

In the end, we made it. Absolutely freezing, I didn't get time to put my gloves on; I didn't want to let go or stop progress, so I just held on in the bitter snowy wind around his waist. As we drove into the last stretch of harbour, I slipped into the chest-deep water just behind where the waves were breaking on the concrete slipway. The relative warmth of the water being slightly better than the air was good news to my paws! The slipway was being surged by big storm waves, so we had to time it and drag the ski up out of the surges before we could trailer it. Hanno slipped in, and we timed a surge in the waves to run with and pull the ski with us. I was on one side near the bow, and he on the other. As a wave passed below and began to break, I slipped my frozen fingers up under the edge of the ski and started to run with the surge dragging the ski along until we were high and dry on the concrete. I let go momentarily to flex my frozen sausage-like fingers for a second before the next surge came, and once again I jammed the sausages into the groove below the bow and dragged it a little further to be clear of the surf. Once we were back ashore, I felt like my arms stopped at my wrists. My fingers were sharp with cold. It made me begin to hunch over in pain. My hands were completely frozen, but I had to carry on.

Instead of getting changed and getting completely soaked in my clothes in the snow, I tried to wriggle my dead hands into my neoprene gloves as I knew I had another 10 minutes of this to get the ski on the trailer, and at least they would protect me from the wind for a while. Hanno ran up the slip to get the van and trailer and began to reverse down a little closer. The slip even had snow on it, so we couldn't risk reversing all the way down. I grabbed a rope from the hatch of the ski and attached it to the trailer and then to Hanno's tow hitch with the biggest stupidest knots I've ever tied with hands that didn't work properly. This gave us about 30 feet of space and meant the van didn't need to come down to the edge of the surf. We slipped the trailer under the front of the ski, and Hanno began to winch. I was at the stern, leaning into the ski to help it onto the trailer with my forearms so as not to have to bend my stone-cold wrists and hands. Once it was on, Hanno gently pulled the ski up the slip with the van, and it was time to get changed! My feet were then also frozen, as were Hanno's. The wind cutting through the neoprene with ease. I was trying to remove skin tight neoprene boots from frozen feet with frozen sausage-like fingers and swollen hands. I had to use brute force and ignorance to make any progress and ended up momentarily standing in the snow on concrete in bare feet before taking my entire kit off in one full move. I decided it better to go through the pain of using frozen fingers once to remove all my stuff than to stop and start, so within seconds, I was bollock naked on a concrete slip standing in the snow. I couldn't feel my feet, and it felt like I no longer had hands, but I started to giggle at the thought of anyone coming down the road to the harbour that might see me in the nip like a snowman with a bright red head, a really warm see-through white body, big red feet, and blue hands!

I'm used to having cold hands; in fact, it never really bothers me too much. My body never gets cold, but the extremities do once they are exposed to the wind chill. It was horrific. My body wasn't cold at all, but my hands felt so bad. I remember as a kid coming up the beach at Castlerock and discovering that putting cold hands in warm water is the most painful thing I could do to them. Instead, I used to fill the sink with cold tap water and warm them up in it! Sometimes the swelling wouldn't go down for over a day!

Although we were then dry and safely ashore, we had to go and get our boards back. The blizzard still pushing in hard. I had my rigger boots on and all my clothes. To get the boards, we had to drive about two miles and then walk down a long road to the beach and then another three-quarters of a mile to where they were stashed. I didn't want to leave them overnight just cos poor wee Alastair had cold hands! We drove to the top of the hill and abandoned the van and ski there as we probably wouldn't get back up out of the car park in the snow. We decided we were going to run the entire way there and back to get warmed up. So, laden in all my clothes and boots and a ski jacket, I began to run down the hill. Running down hill is such a bitch and even worse in the snow. As soon as I got to the frozen sand, it was much easier to keep momentum. We moved up into the pathway running behind the dunes until we got to the boards – two 9kg weighted tow boards. Hanno took one, and I took the other. Sweating like maniacs, we began to run back, hands once again exposed to the elements as the wind howled and snow continued to fall. I had to keep going now. My hands had just warmed up enough to grip the board, and then I put them back into the wind for a 2k run! If hands could think, they would be thinking *that big shite is taking the piss out of us now*! We eventually got back to the van after dark, and the main road was completely covered in snow. A tractor passed by, and the farmer gave us a look of *wtf are you two doing with a jet ski in tow and two surfboards*! All this came from one tiny moment, making us unstable, and capsizing!

This is exactly why I get so anxious and scared for everyone at times, and I'm so hard on them in training. I regularly shout and drill rescues and driving techniques repeatedly. This was one of Hanno's first times in big whitewater with a ski. These silly little things of minute detail can cause massive problems when on a real mission, so it's better to get them out of the way on a training day. This could have been a lot worse, way out at sea, or one of us could have been seriously hurt by the ski when we came off in the surf. As bad as it was, we survived it this time. Good consistent team training reduces all sorts of unknown issues if we can deal with them or have been through them in training. When Hanno first started with me, he used to lose the jet ski several times in training sessions, everyone does for that matter. Every time I looked around, he was swimming after the ski. Eventually, he stopped losing it. Knowing that he grew out of it means I trust in him as a team member on big days.

I've trained him through all the way to being expert on the ski. If one of us loses it, I know he and all of us have had experience together in retrieving it, working on it as best we can, and ultimately getting back to shore safely. The more things like that for me that happen in training, the more time I have to focus on the good stuff, imagining, visualising myself and all the guys charging huge waves, so that when it comes to the day, we have dealt with as many things well in advance and reduced the level of unknown quantities as possible. Therefore, we reduce our anxiety and fear of several potential situations unfolding, ultimately meaning that none of us should ever panic. It leads to better performance of us as individuals and us as a team.

17

BACK ON THE HORSE FEAR

It's a dark grim day on the west coast of Ireland. Where normally it's possible to stand on a headland and see the horizon, thick grey drizzle clogs the view appearing to block everything except the path of 50-foot monsters marching out of the North Atlantic and detonating on the shallow rock ledge just off the coast at Mullaghmore head. Darkness is setting in at 3 p.m. and within the next two hours, it will be pitch black.

I'm out the back of the headland floating in the dark inky blue water, heart thumping. The stress I feel at this moment is incredible at times. I'm waiting on my tow partner, Paul, to pull me up on the rope using his jet ski and drive me into the path of one of these beasts. He is standing tall on the ski watching like a hawk trying to see through the drizzle and huge lumps of swell marching towards us. I'm on my honkers in the water, feet strapped into my bright orange tow board. My breathing is short and restricted by my life jackets, and I'm trying to calm myself down and get some air into my lungs by inhaling and exhaling as best I can to get a full lungful of air and try to calm the jitters. The last thing I need is to be going on a bomb with not much air. I momentarily glance up to the headland in the distance and notice the wet black tarmac hill running down to the edge of the cliff between the fields is streaming with water from all the rain. The few conspicuous palm trees standing their ground at the top of the hill. Paul calls over the wind, and it's time to go. He pulls me up, and we begin tracking parallel to a huge dark wall of North Atlantic juice coming at us from the west. Now that my torso is above the waterline, I quickly try to get a few good breathes in. I'm going through all sorts of things in my head at light speed. Hoping he times it right, hoping I'm not too deep and get smashed, hoping I'm deep enough that I get a good scary ride, but not too scary.

It's getting steeper and steeper, and we are going faster and faster as he expertly positions me right in the spot before angling the ski for the safety of the edge of the wave. Paul always drives well; he is extremely good at it and gives me or anyone he tows with great confidence. I lean on the rope to give me a final squirt, let go, and I'm gone. Just me and this beast now; I grit my teeth and lean forward heading down into the thing. My board is running smoothly as the wave steepens, and I pass the point of no return. I'm completely focused, no fear, no emotion. I go into a tunnel vision-like state where I only seem to see a very narrow field in front of me. Very little noise ever registers with me, but my senses are obviously working overtime subconsciously. I'm over the ledge now, and the rocks below start to drain as I hurtle down the wave as it grows bigger and taller above me. I am going so fast I can't get an edge to turn the board, and I know I'm f£$ked.

In a split second, I need to decide to try and outrun the 40-foot wall of water that is about to detonate regardless of my decision ... or bail. I don't think I have enough speed to get in front of the explosion despite going fast, and I can't get an edge, so I decide to step out of my straps and not risk getting smashed through my board by a sledgehammer lip. I take a quick look up over my right shoulder and then over my left. I'm right below the thing like a sitting duck. I step off; I see the wave pass my face just before impact, and I get rag dolled beyond belief. My helmet fills with water, and it's like King Kong has me in one hand shaking the life out of me, trying to pull my head off. I try to cover up and go with it, but the forces won't let me keep my limbs in around myself. Something glances off my head, and I'm not sure if it was my board or the rock ledge. I'm underwater worrying that I've been down so long now the next wave might be right there when I surface, and I won't get a breath before the next beating. Eventually, it releases me, and I begin to work my way to the surface as fast as I can, but there is so much water above me it takes me an age to break above the surface. My shitty lifejacket is struggling under the pressure. I'm trying to get to the surface quickly without panic setting in. I surface and take a gulp of air, but there is froth everywhere trying to swamp me. Everything is white; Paul knows I'm down and is looking for me. My vision is blurred, and I can't hear properly. I have my arm up in the air, so he can see me, but so much froth obscures me from his view. My vision is blurred and I can't hear properly. The next wave breaks with extreme force, and I've nowhere to run. I prepare for another beating. The huge wall of whitewater is exploding and rushing towards me like a double decker bus. It hits full force, and I go through the mill again. This time I surface, and another crew comes to get me.

It was obviously bad enough looking that they decided to come in for me. I was battered, my helmet cracked, and my board gone. Paul came over, found my board, and I got onto the ski with him. I was f£$ked. Totally depleted of energy and oxygen in just a few minutes of ocean-driven violence. But, I knew I needed to go again. I don't remember feeling scared at this point, I was just determined to go. I had only one thing on my mind, and I needed to do it now. I took a short breather, slipped back into the water with the sole focus of not letting this get to me. I wasn't scared but knew that over time I may dwell on it, so I needed to get back on the horse right away. Paul drove me onto two more beasts. I didn't fully commit on them, but it was enough to prevent the feeling of finishing the day on that wipeout, and then wishing I had gone back for more for weeks, months, or until the next winter. Of course, I took a risk in getting back on the horse so soon after such a beating, but I figured it a lesser of two evils over what I may go through psychologically if I didn't. I went to the hospital for a concussion checkup. At that time, it was the worst beating I had. It's something as a big wave surfer I've always known was coming, but just never known when. I've always feared it and how bad the next bad wipeout will be. But it doesn't stop me. Yes, I may surf slightly more cautiously or conservatively in the huge waves with it in mind than if I wasn't scared or trying to avoid that. The acceptance of the eventuality that at some point I'm going to get a rattling beyond what I have had so far has become the norm for me. I've been doing this a very long time, and wipeouts or beatings or hold downs have got progressively worse, more violent, more injurious, more intimidating. I'm sure if a doctor analyzed me, I probably have some sort of post-traumatic stress at times. I get hit hard and violently on occasion – I suppose like a car crash. I was once monitored by a sports science company called Statsports, and they discovered that the impacts I have in some wipeouts are equal to that of a 70-mph car crash. Also in one average big wave session, I get hit more and as hard as the highest impact of the 15 players on a rugby field do in one game! That has got to leave a mark in the mind of some description in my subconscious. I can count less than a handful of incidents in the surf where it's stuck with me all my life. Most involve sudden

177

impact that although I am always shocked by it, it's not the hold down or the impact itself that frightens me when I'm deep underwater, it's the violence. The violence of the whitewater smashing deep below the surface, the energy bouncing off the reef back towards the surface and me somewhere in the middle of all that, is frightening at times. It's ripped my wetsuit zipper open, removed my boots and my lifejackets at times. Kind of like getting mauled by a wild animal and then crawling back to hide with clothes in tatters wondering what the f£$k I was doing in the lion's pen anyway.

18

TECHNIQUES

Being scared is largely seen as being a bad thing and often leads to under performance or not being able to do something. I've found it to be the opposite. It all depends how you look at it. Being scared is perfectly normal; it's our safety mechanism, and it warns us of our approaching limits to let us know to prepare for pushing them and prevent us going into uncontrollable panic. Or you could argue that fear is there to warn us of danger and that we need to know this is as far as we can go now, and we must turn our plans around. It's all in the way you look at it. It's never clear cut or as simple as that in reality, but that is the basis of how I deal with fear.

179

I've heard and read several things about techniques that apparently work involving controlled breathing, counting etc, that stuff has never worked for me. I tried that a few times, and all that does is make me focus on my breathing and my heart rate going mad; it doesn't help me achieve anything, it just makes things worse for me taking my mind away from what I want to do to focus on something else. I find it makes me think only of my breathing and heart, the side effects of the fear or anxiety, instead of dealing with the thing causing it and makes things worse. It distracts me from what I'm trying to do. I use a few different techniques to combat anxiety and fear. Both the feelings are very different, but they can be related to the same thing. I like to gather as much information as I can about anything that is causing me to be anxious or scared. The unknown element is usually the thing causing any sort of fear for me. The more I can learn about it, the more I can diminish its effects, eliminate it and move forward. In the heat of the moment I usually use anger and vocals to push me through the fear and allow me to do the thing I am trying to achieve. I find that in a nutshell, if there is something either in surfing or in some other walk of life coming up in the future, the best thing to do is to educate myself. Find out everything I can, that way there are less chances for little surprises to knock me off track in the moment. But, when it comes to the heat of the moment fear, it might be sudden, it might have been planned but either way I find anger and loud vocals to be the most effective. I find it happens instinctively. A good auld shout or growl does wonders and focusses me in the moment of going over the line of no return so to speak. Thankfully it's only a very rare occasion that I have to do this!

19

ANGER

There is something to be said for using anger to subdue fear. If I think through all the situations in which I've been scared right at the brink of something about to happen in real life or in the final split seconds before I catch a big wave, I usually mutter something aggressively under my breath or at times even growl or shout! When fear shows its face, one of the most effective ways to get action to happen is through anger. Fear can freeze us to the spot, make us stunned, not think straight. Anger snaps me out of it. For example, just today, I used a strong flowing river mouth to squirt me out to sea past the breaking waves at Castlerock. The flow was heavy with snow runoff in the water, a dead low tide, and 50 mph south-west winds. I use this technique regularly on big days, but today I got spat way out to sea in the flow and had to paddle back ashore against it. My mind was running through all sorts of things and eventualities whilst my arms were going strong and steady driving me through it. When this happens, I think about when I paddled a surfboard to Scotland for charity predominantly against the tide. I start to call myself names and get angry with myself to the point of total stubbornness, and I begin to fight beyond where my mind and body was letting me a few minutes earlier. It works – the anger causes me to fight. There used to be a Viking army called The Berserkers. The word we use, 'Berserk' is derived from their name. They were apparently famous for shouting, growling, beating their chests, and getting really worked up before battle. Clearly a tactic used to combat fear and allow them into harm's way. Big wave surfing is a discipline in which we put ourselves in harm's way. The mind is in turmoil, scared and confused as to why it is doing this to itself when it knows it could get hurt or worse. I find I go into a deathly calm before the moment I am about to turn and go for a wave, but quite often that includes cursing through gritted teeth and at times a proper growl! I have also been known to be sitting astride my board frozen with fear and thump my chest and again, "Come on you F$%^&* F%^&$£% let's do this!" Clearly a primitive natural response to handling fear and still being able to put myself in places and situations my rational mind is disagreeing with.

20

THE THRESHOLD OF FEAR

I talk about this thing called the Threshold of Fear to people all the time. This threshold I refer to is the point at which fear kicks in and comfort starts to dwindle, or in some cases, jump out a window. To be honest, in big wave surfing it's an extremely difficult thing to maintain because it may be that I only get the opportunity to ride big waves in the depth of winter despite being prepared all year. I then build the threshold of fear higher through the winter months, and just as I've really pushed my comfort level, spring arrives, the winter storms and swells leave, and my fear threshold drops off over the seasons until winter comes around again. This

185

means that it takes a long time to become a very confident operator in big seas.

However, almost every other pursuit in the world or thing we need to face is not reliant on the seasons and in lots of cases can be done daily. If the thing you fear or are anxious about can be done regularly, or even as much as daily, then I truly believe you have a very strong chance of dealing with the fear that is stopping you doing it if it's something you really want. For me, the more exposure I have to big waves, the more comfortable I get, the more confident I get. Therefore, the higher the Threshold of Fear becomes, I begin to operate in a much more calm and controlled state of mind, able to push harder than before in bigger and bigger waves. The same is true in a lot of areas in life. As I have said earlier in this book, I am not a doctor or health professional, and I speak only of my own experience here and knowing what I have done to overcome certain situations, allowing me to progress in the areas of my life that I want to. I hope that people can take something from my experience in a big or small way that will allow them to develop their own personal approach to handling their fears and anxieties to progress in whatever they are pursuing.

21

BE A WARRIOR

Imagine this was 100s of years ago. The world was arguably much simpler. Men fought in battles and wars with bare hands and improvised or hand-made weapons. They didn't have infrared sight and automatic machinegun fire to allow them to operate from a distance without seeing the whites of their opponents' eyes.

If they were overcome by fear, would they survive? No. One of the main reasons they fought not just their opponent but their fear in doing so was a lack of other choices. They had to. They didn't have someone to bail them out, someone to phone and tell they couldn't do something today for whatever reason; they didn't have an alternative other than to defend what they had, their families, and where they lived. They didn't have emergency services to call upon. If their father was killed, they picked up the sword and kept fighting on, scared or not.

It seems like people today have become so lost in all the chaos of the world's advancements that those basic instincts of fighting through fear for survival have in some cases been smothered. I speak here not in the form of physical fighting (unless completely necessary of course), but a lot can be drawn from those men back then and brought into our everyday lives.

I used to compete on The UK Pro Surf Tour. I really struggled at the beginning for lots of reasons. I knew I was at an immediate disadvantage by being so much bigger than most other surfers in the usually very small competition waves. This, combined with a few other things, at times made me freeze up, and I literally had rings surfed around me in heats where I knew I was a better surfer than the guys beating me, but I just couldn't snap out of it. I totally froze up to the point I may as well not have entered the events. It drove me to tears at one point and then drove me to become an extremely focused machine fixated on getting over this problem and letting myself do it!

It got to the point I was driving home from a contest in Wales in heavy rain in the winter, and I couldn't stop thinking about how badly I was surfing and that I was letting myself down and anyone who had believed in me. I stopped the car, phoned home, and I was crying and totally distraught at what a complete disgrace I was being to myself.

That was the turning point. I went home, and I immersed myself in it all. I realised that I was being out-surfed because I was not surfing at home where I was the big fish in the little pond; I was among other guys who could surf, and I wasn't used to seeing this all the time. I was kind of mesmerised by it, and it made me second guess myself to the point I didn't surf. I just sat there on my board watching everything around me, frozen to the spot.

I went home and worked out the exact reasons for me being like this. I wrote down what they were and what I needed to do to change them.

I then wrote down everything I knew I was capable of.

I went way deeper than that, though. I wrote positive things on A4 paper around my room and went and saw a hypnotherapist and started reading sports psychology and listening to subliminal psychology tapes. I recorded affirmations on my Dictaphone and played it over to myself in the bath each night. I knew it wasn't my surfing ability that was holding me back, it was my mindset and freezing up scared to perform. So, I tackled my mind and head intensely, and it worked! I started surfing like myself; I worked on training my mind as much as my body, and I started surfing to the best of my ability again in contests. Going back to the warrior mindset, I used to visualize myself as a warrior facing my opponents on a battlefield. Not in the surf but on a battlefield. It made me put them into perspective as people not as surfers, and it led me to winning heats over them as I had already dealt with facing them in my mind, and they were nothing to me once I entered the surf.

This started me on a path of facing all sorts of things head on knowing I was capable of it. From emotional things to family, friends, enemies, surfing, life in general. In a short space of time, I had educated myself and given myself the tools to be able to tackle anything, and I wasn't scared to get a clobbering in the process. I committed, I accepted.

22

BIG BLUE

It's 3.30 a.m. My street is deserted. The orange light of the street lamps the only colour of warmth. I'm standing in my garage doorway wrapped up in a million layers of clothes. My breath clearly visible in the stillness and icy air. The usual sound of water dripping outside completely absent. I'm having one last look to make sure I haven't forgotten anything. The garage is a clutter of everything from tools, to weight training equipment, martial arts gear, two boats, three trailers, wetsuits, clothes, 50-odd surfboards, and God knows what else. Literally a lifetime of equipment. The van is backed up to the door with its rear doors open. Everything from huge surfboards strapped to the ceiling, to spare vehicle parts, tools, firewood, extra clothes, spare wetsuits, it's all neatly placed in the van in a selection of multi-coloured fishing boxes I've salvaged from the shoreline over the years. I roll the garage shutter down slowly so as not to wake the neighbours. I pour the leftover water from the kettle that I didn't put in my flask over the windscreen to clear the ice. I push the van out of the street and once I'm around the corner, I jump in, close the door, and pray that it starts. I have an old van – I always worry it might not start on a cold morning. I carry a jumpstart kit and a mains charger pack, just in case. I put the key in the ignition, hold my breath, and she fires up into life. It's on; here we go! My first port of call is just 30 seconds away at my friend Hanno's house, just around the corner. As I arrive, he is in his driveway, setting all his gear out ready to load into the van. The air is still, the sky clear and stars blanketed across the night sky. It's extremely unusual; normally, there is a strong south-west wind – it just hasn't arrived yet is my thinking. I pause to take a quick look at the wave buoy data on my phone to discover the swell has arrived; it's grown through the night on the buoy moored on the edge of the continental shelf. Usually what shows there the night before makes landfall in the morning, and if it's still showing size in the morning on the buoy, then I know we are in for huge waves all day. We are leaving early to make sure we have room for error, room for problems on the road, ice, or if we have any vehicle trouble. All being well, we should arrive before sunrise. Hanno loads the rest of his gear into the van, and we pull off. We operate a tight ship; we don't have time to let 10 minutes slip by when we are on a mission. There is a strong air of excitement, anticipation, nerves, and quiet confidence between us.

I have been doing this for most of my life. I know the thrills, the adrenaline, and the dangers well. I've worked with various people over the years in pursuit of huge waves. It takes a special mindset to want to pursue giant waves in the North Atlantic in cold isolated locations, and it's not for everyone. Some people think it's for them until they hear the waves exploding, suffer the violence of a wipeout, have the fright of their lives. Others have all of that and stand strong, push on, surrender never. It's a special thing – it breeds camaraderie, breeds passion, breeds teamwork and creates memories and stories that go down in history. It takes a special mind to want this; it isn't like anywhere else in the world, and risk is at a premium. I won't do this with just anyone – I happily sit swells out if I don't have the right minds around me. These people are special. Together, we can do what appears superhuman to the onlooker, we can take risks beyond what an individual can handle as we are tightly trained, and we all know that no man gets left behind, no matter what. We all go out, and we all come home. Calculated Madness. On this day, it's just Hanno and I, and we are meeting Charles at the border to convoy the rest of the way. We haven't brought jet skis or safety drivers this time. No one else was available, but we want to paddle some huge waves, so we have to make do with just the three of us. That's OK, though, we have prepared for that, and we are well used to being on our own.

We notice the hedges are blowing around now, trees swinging at the roadside as the van headlights whizz by. There is a nervous silence in the van as we visualize what that means at the spot we are going to, far out at sea. Anxiety is in the air; the unknown factor of the ever-changing elements is on our minds. One thing you can rely on here is that the weather forecast is unreliable! We were so happy to have no wind as we left Portrush, but now we have had a reality check; the chaos is coming, and within a couple of hours we will be far offshore in this wind trying to ride huge waves among chop the size of a family car.

We normally start off chatty in the morning, then as we get further down the road, silence creeps in as we start to ponder what we might be in for in a few hours. I go through similar emotions and thoughts as I do when I'm completely on my own, but when there is a team of us, and we have jet skis and two vans, there is a lot going on in my mind. I worry about the skis breaking down. I worry about each of the guys. I worry that they will be scared or get hurt... I worry a lot. There's only the two of us going in the water today, so I'm not feeling too uneasy. The inclusion of engines has its benefits at times, but they do add extra stress and organization too, and sometimes just a couple of us paddling is more enjoyable even if it is less safe.

I don't ever properly settle down until I'm in the sea, in the middle of it all. Strangely, that's when I'm most at ease. I probably worry about all these things because I know what can happen. I know the consequences when something goes wrong. And, that's the thing with this. I know something will go wrong – it's part of it. It's not undue worry because this is the wild Atlantic, and we cannot expect to get away unscathed all the time in the process of chasing huge waves. Something will go wrong, it always does; it just depends to what degree it will be.

We are usually isolated, and we only have ourselves to rely on, so we need to be super tight, well-trained and know exactly what each other is capable of at the moment something goes wrong. Today is going to be our biggest day to date, it's scary, it's exciting, and we are a little anxious, but we feed off each other and keep moving forward.

We meander down the last couple of miles from up in the mountains, the icy roads left high up behind us. The last mile is the most anxious, and we cruise along the lane trying to get a clear peek at the sea. Is it big? Is the wind good? A mixture of anxiety and panic runs through us as we wonder what will be on offer when we round the last corner into the layby and get our first look out to sea.

Hanno jumps out, old receipts blow across the dashboard as the cold wind sweeps through the open door and through my open window. The sea is dark; the spray looks whiter than white against the deep rolling swell as the tops of waves whipped up into the air fill the scene with a ghostly mist drifting above the lines of clean slow rolling swell. The sea is in mountains, the horizon like a dark hole in the distance, lumpy and unruly. The wind stiff offshore. We scamper up the knoll for a slightly better vantage point. Vapour fills the bay, and huge waves are exploding at various spots for as far as the eye can see. Out there in the distance, a behemoth subsea rock ledge lies in the path of unsuspecting open ocean swell ready to trip it up and send it toppling to its icy Irish death. That's where we are heading, to catch and ride one of those beasts in its moments before imminent beautiful demise and destruction. Behind us, our van loaded with all our gear for a mission unlike any other. The cold air drifts from our exhales just as it does from the exploded waves all around us. The anticipation of what we are going to see when we start to head way out to sea is frightening and extremely exciting. As we stand on this slight rise in terrain close to boulders and outcrops with 40-foot waves detonating all around us, it feels like we are in no man's land. Very few words are spoken as we gaze around the scene taking it all in; it's everything we dreamed of. It's all led to this moment. I feel the air of nervousness. I have felt this a million times; I know I need to let Hanno have his head space too, to absorb it all, but it's time to go.

"Let's go," I state and turn and back down the hill towards the van. Hanno leaves his gaze on the hill and follows me. It's time to do this. The silence is incredible. Riding huge waves is imminent; it's about to happen, time to suit up and man up. Something brought us together to do this, here we are, and it's time. We drive a little further south down the coast, continually pointing and gasping at waves breaking all along the coast at several spots. We come to a narrow lane that traverses the coastline across peat bog and rock and brings us to an open field. We carefully drive across the field so as not to get bogged down. Both vehicles pull up and stop. We park right in front of a wave I first surfed in 2003. It breaks just off the coast across a dangerous channel over a submerged reef. The tide is too full for it to break properly at this moment, but we are planning on surfing one of the other four spots in the bay to the north. The sky is completely clear and blue; the wind is dropping, and the swell monstrous.

The spot we are planning on surfing is normally accessible from a much better location, but the surf is so big, the entire rocky shoreline is being smashed by huge, relentless, unforgiving walls of whitewater giving us no way out. We have only one option to get out there, and it is going to involve a few extra risks. The waves we plan to surf break over a rock ledge to the north. The area has a notorious south to north current, so we know we will get pushed up the coast quickly, which is OK until we must come back! Today, we are going to jump off a cliff into a tiny protected bay behind an outcrop of rock. From there, we must time our exit from that bay and sneak by a dry rock slab on the northern headland without getting dragged into it by the current.

Any heat that was in the van from the journey has gone, the cold wind blowing from the icy mountains sweeps through. We both start to pull our stuff out. We take a little corner each outside the van next to an open door to set our clothes as we get changed. There is no space inside, so we stand outside trying to milk any protection from the biting wind behind ajar van doors. It's a complete psychological battle at this point. There is no heat; we are tired and going through an energy dump. Getting into a freezing wetsuit in a field right now is not easy. I sheepishly pull off a boot, then a sock, and stand on the empty boot. I do the same with the next one. I'm trying my hardest not to stand on the frosty grass on which we are parked. I whip off my jeans and tracksuit bottoms I have underneath in one go, baring all to the wind. I wriggle one foot into my suit whilst trying to balance on my empty boots. As I slip the next big white slab of freezing foot into the other leg of the suit, I stumble and end up standing in the crunchy white grass cursing myself! I quickly haul the suit up to my waist as I jump back onto the empty boots. I slip my feet into my wetsuit boots, and suddenly everything seems warm. The thick neoprene clings tightly to my lower half, and I feel no cold; in fact, my mood has lifted, and I'm feeling ready to do this. I keep my top layer on as I go to the rear of the van where Hanno is huddled into the doorway going through a similar battle in the mind.

He has his suit to his waist and is now bare chested to the elements but looks unfazed as he sets his clothes neatly in the van. I reach by him and pull a black board bag containing a very special piece of equipment from the ceiling of the van. My favourite board, a 10'8" big wave gun. It's red and white and was made by my friend Rosy. I've caught probably my best big waves on this board. It has the scars of travel, the marks of wear and tear, and the wounds of battle after surviving 10 winters of big wave riding since it was built. I lay it on the grass and pull it out of the bag. Its bright colours stand out against the desaturated muted colours of the morning. I have over 50 surfboards; if they could speak, they would have some amazing tales to tell. I put the board bag back in the van, whip all my upper layers off in one go, hurl them over Hanno's head into the back of the van, and wriggle into the rest of my suit.

My family has a lot of seamen on my dad's side. I know more superstitions from the sea than you can imagine, and over time I've unintentionally developed my own. I won't let anyone zip up my wetsuit, – I always must do it myself, no matter how cold my hands are or whatever is stuck in the zipper. I will shout at anyone who reaches a friendly hand out to help. No bananas come to sea with us, no mention of pigs, pork, sausages and several other obscure things that would rarely be on our tongue anyway but have stuck with me through my time and inherited from family and fellow seamen over the years. Before I enter, and just as I leave the water, I close my eyes and nod to the horizon and for a quick moment think of everyone with me, loved ones and of people who may be looking over us and our equipment. I'm not religious or spiritual, but it's something I've always done for some reason.

The silence is still thick between us. No one has really said a word since we arrived, other than the odd grunt as we get geared. Everyone is in their own head space, their own mind, trying to keep the anxiety down. Charles is checking out vantage points to shoot from with the light and spray in the air knowing that we are going to be a long way from him and losing sight of us a strong possibility. We don't even know how big it's going to be out there; we have all sorts of things running through our minds. These are the biggest waves we have tackled together yet, and paddling with no jet ski back up, I'm worried about us both. I'm thinking about what Hanno is thinking, what Charles is thinking. I'm trying to visualize myself surfing, dealing with chop, speed, the current, prepare my mind. I'm hoping Hanno has the nerve to commit in the final moment and not hesitate; I'm hoping he feels ready.

We put on our layers of impact and float protection and cover up in a bright colour so we can spot each other more clearly. I'm in red and Hanno in yellow, with Charles in a bright hat, so hopefully, we can see him from a distance at sea back ashore too. I text my mate Simon, our location coordinates, crew members, an estimated time of arrival back ashore of 3 p.m. He texts back to confirm receipt, and that he will call for back-up if no word received after 3.30 p.m. That gives us room for error, but we know he is on the case if we have an issue at sea.

Hanno is going to surf an 8'6" board. We pick our boards off the grass and begin to walk with Charles along the coast a little further to the north where there is a cliff face down into slightly protected waters. This little bay is the only place we can safely get into the water and not get pummeled by whitewater. However, it has its own dangers. Being a small bay, when the swells surge into it, that water drains back out so although we know we will get spat out of it quickly past a shallow rock ledge with a crazy wave smashing into it, we know that coming back we may have trouble. Our back-up plan should something go wrong is to paddle north to one of the other spots and attempt to get ashore through huge lines of whitewater which eventually dissipate and break onto a stony shoreline as opposed to a rock outcrop shoreline. If we have to do that, then we will most likely have surrendered to the current or something has happened, and we need to get ashore quickly in whatever way we can. It's not a great back-up option, but it's all we have.

Charles stands slightly higher above us and tells us to be careful. I'm trying to find a spot in the water that doesn't have a rock below that I can jump cleanly into. I jump with my board under my right arm from the 20-foot cliff. As I hit the water, I let my board go so as not to be hit by it. Hanno lands right in behind me. We sit up on our boards, take a quick breather, gather our thoughts, and then get paddling into the flow. We are swept quickly out of the bay. We hug the southernmost side of the bay to try and avoid the huge waves breaking just across from us. Once clear of both headlands, we start to paddle north. There are four big wave peaks to the north in our path, and we are paddling to the first. We don't want to go as far as the second because it is a slightly more disorganised wave, and with no back-up, we want to play it relatively safe especially considering how big the swell is. There is a series of underwater ledges running along this coastline. In some places, the rock ledge sits closer to the surface than others and causes huge deep ocean swells to trip up as they march towards the coast causing them to topple, spill, and explode with violence over the rock ledge. That's where we want to be. Sitting in the path of those swells, over the rock ledge trying to keep our cool to be in position to ride one of those beasts as it approaches its final moments and prepares for its imminent demise upon the lurking ledge of rock just below the surface.

We are getting swept up the coast quickly. When I first surfed out here in 2003 at the wave in the southern end of the bay, I remember thinking the current was strong. It pulled me past the spot I wanted to be at and almost resulted in my safety driver losing the boat he was driving cos the current had moved him directly into the peak of the spot over the shallowest part of the reef and had him breaching the top of a couple of huge unexpected waves.

We kept paddling. We stopped the odd time to check our position and could see Charles gradually disappearing into the distance obscured by spray and a very low brightly shining reflection of the sun on the water's surface.

As we paddled, we kept seeing these big blue wobbly peaks coming out of deep water and toppling onto the reef. The current was running through them, making them wobble and move around as they approached. We knew we were going to be paddling a lot to hold position.

As we got to the spot, we looked ashore; we could no longer see Charles behind a mixture of low sun glare, sea spray and mist, and unruly passing swell. We located two little white cottages up on the hillside a few miles away and lined them up with another towards the foot of the hill. We had no mark ups laterally as the island in the distance was too low lying and the headland to the north juts out on its own with nothing to cross reference it to. The big waves were infrequent, which was good and bad. The infrequency meant we would at times be sitting in relatively calm water, and then out of nowhere the horizon would disappear, and these huge blue lines would start marching in, and we would be scrambling to find position to try and catch them or run from them.

We were both feeling good; it was big, but it didn't feel life-threateningly so. I was feeling very confident. We were continually checking our position and trying to stay upstream of the current. It took us about 20 minutes to get here, and I feared going back might be a struggle, so we agreed that we would both aim to catch one big wave and then make our way back. We aimed to minimize the risk, but by focusing on catching bombs, we would maximise our experiences.

I managed to sneak onto an average-sized wave; it was bumpy, and I struggled to stay on as I hurtled down the big blue face of the wave. I wanted more, and my plan to just catch one went out the window quickly as I paddled back out.

This was the biggest paddle day Hanno had been out in with me at this stage. I knew he was probably feeling a little nervous. However, after I caught that one, he was bang in position to catch a pretty big one. The big blue line of water was wobbling its way from the North Atlantic with his name on it, and it was coming directly for him. There was a lot of current making it choppy, but he swung his board around and scrambled into its path and took off. I paddled up over the shoulder of the wave as the white spray began to cap, and he disappeared over the ledge and down into the bottom of the big blue wave and out of my sight. I was swamped by spray raining down on me as I turned to watch the back of the wave that he was on pushing towards the coast. Then to my right, he appeared up over the shoulder, silhouetted against the sunlight and the spray. He made it!

Next, it was my turn. The biggest one yet was approaching, and I was lucky enough to be right in front of it. I remember seeing all the chop on it as it wobbled its way towards me and thinking, *I won't be able to get any momentum up in my paddling to get enough speed to catch it with so much chop.* I was paddling parallel to the incoming line of water, trying to get myself away from being right in below the peak as I knew I was too deep and was going to get clobbered. I was not sure if I was going to make it out of the way never mind catch it, and I was paddling fast towards the shoulder. At the very last minute, there was a little bit of chop that broke at the very top, and I immediately and instinctively spun my board towards shore and took a few deep strokes as I stared down the face of this big blue beast about to detonate onto the reef. I could see Hanno in the distance paddling back out, and as the whitewater clipped me at the very top of the wave, I stood up. I could see I was in for a rough ride and set a wide stance ready to wrestle my 10'8" down this thing. I went over a little ledge which sent me almost airborne, but I managed to regain control and the board went effortlessly over the next lump as the wave started to draw water off the reef and smooth out all the bumps. I felt totally in control, and as I dropped down the face, I slipped the board onto its left edge to allow me to be straight down the bottom and in the middle of the peak. It was a beautiful big blue wave, and I rode it all the way down to the bottom where I was rushed by the whitewater but not knocked off. I pulled up over the shoulder and kicked out at the end of the ride as my board started to slow down and was about to come to a complete stop. I let myself go weightless and drop backwards into the water. I was ecstatic. The sun was shining, the sea was blue with a huge swell, and beautiful, bright whitewater, and there we were just the two of us trading waves with McQuillan in the distance keeping an eye on us.

It was time to go, we had spent a couple of hours out there, and we got what we came for. There was no point trying to better our rides when we had a lot of elements against us. If we drifted in the current to the north any further, we would be in real trouble trying to get ashore, and if anything happened to either of us, we would be in a difficult situation far out at sea.

We were both ecstatic, but we had a big paddle to do now, so it was time to get the head down. We started to make our way south back towards the cliff we jumped off, but the tide was raging, and we were making very little headway. It was at the point that if we stopped paddling, we would lose ground. It was like paddling up a watery escalator the wrong way.

The reason the current is so strong here is because there is an island chain to the south that the tide fills, and when the tide drains, the water largely funnels out this narrow gap between the most northerly island and the mainland causing a bottleneck effect and the flow to increase in speed.

So, we are paddling against that. It gets more and more difficult the closer we get to where we jumped off. Charles' silhouette becomes visible on the clifftop as he stands in front of the low winter sun. I'm sure he is watching us through his big lens. He has seen me out in all sorts of conditions, so he is probably able to tell we are having to fight hard this time to get back. I break away from Hanno a little; I didn't leave him behind, but I deliberately opened a bit of a gap. Sometimes I think when one person can get out in front, it helps moral and makes everyone fight harder. I got to the mouth of the little bay after about 40 minutes, and he was maybe 100 yards behind me. I realised the currents at the bay were a lot worse than when we set off. The slab of rock on the northern side was being pounded by 30-

foot behemoths and exploding into the air sending white spray up into the blue sky. I knew if I tried to go into the bay, I would most likely be washed into that wave, so I kept my head down and battled the current further to the south until I was just clear of the southern tip of the bay. I was now being pushed out to sea by the water flowing out of the way. It was incredible. There is a large rocky outcrop – I suppose it's actually an island. The water was running around both sides of it, and waves were coming in from the opposite direction and exploding all over the island making a huge cauldron of whitewater and deep blue water at the same time. I kept checking on Hanno, and he was also persevering in this tidal flow, he was battling hard. I was worried that if we didn't or couldn't fight this, we were going to have to head back to the north and take our chances with the rocky shoreline. I tried to hold my position just out of the bay and waited for a set to approach. I was trying to thread a needle by slipping through the mouth of the bay but not getting smashed onto either the rocky island on the southern end or the slab of rock on the northern end all whilst pushing against the water flowing out of the bay. It was chaotic and frightening to be honest. Charles didn't budge from the headland, keeping a close eye on us. He was only a couple of hundred yards away at this point, up on the cliff. I decided to scramble for it. I had about 200 yards to go; I knew I had to give it my all. I scrambled in alongside the black rocky island as a big swell surged up and over it. The water falling off its side pulled me into the bay and gave me a head start. To my other side, the sound of the waves exploding on the slab alerted me to the fact that there was about to be a lot of water coming back out of this tiny bay any minute now. Suddenly, I hit a brick wall, so to speak. The water started pushing out to sea as if I wasn't there. It was sweeping me back out past the island, and I was paddling like a maniac trying to hold position. Next, another big swell approached from behind and surged over the island and broke on the slab; again, I got pushed into the bay, and this time I paddled even harder, trying to get a little further ahead than last time so as when the bay drained out again, I would be in a slightly better position. It worked. I was now at the back of the island, and as the next big swell began to surge and the bay drained out, I put myself in close to the back of the island, so I couldn't be swept past it, and as the surge from the swell rushed over the island, it then rushed down and onto me pushing me off my board and washing me into the bay! I was safe. I paddled to the side and took refuge behind a big rock and watched as Hanno went through the same thing. Treading water, then getting washed in, and eventually, making it ashore!

Very trying situation, but it was all well worth it! We caught some great big waves! Every time there is a big swell, it's always a mission of some sort, and it involves anxiety beforehand, being worried, scared, intimidated, threatened, and many other emotions. It is extremely draining, and the come down from all that can last up to a week.

23

PREPARING FOR A LIFE OF FACING FEAR - HEALTHY MIND AND BRAIN

Although most of us are fortunate not to have to lift a sword and physically fight every day, we certainly do wield other weapons: our minds, our skills, our careers, our trades, etc. All those things present situations where fear can prevent progression, where fear can breed complacency, where comfort sets in. It is most likely that within one of those everyday things is where there is an issue with some sort of fear, and that's why people read these sorts of books. In order that we are able and willing to operate at our best or as close to our best as we can in the presence of fear, we need to be fit and healthy. After all, quite often we do not know when fear may show up, and we don't have time to go and fuel ourselves, do a quick workout, down a chicken salad or whatever, and be ready to roll. We need to live a healthy life, and that largely centres on diet. Diet fuels our bodies and our minds, allows us to perform in all sorts of ways and recover from trauma, possibly trauma endured during a fearful episode. To plan on tackling fear on a regular basis, then, a good starting place is to tidy up the diet. I'm not talking drastic changes – subtle changes can have a huge effect on attitude, outlook, and positivity when faced with a challenging situation.

Anyone who knows me will know I eat two different diets, not intentionally. I eat extremely well; I look after myself, but I also eat rubbish at times too. I'm extremely active, so maybe I've got away with it so far, but because I eat so well 90% of the time, the times I don't eat well are not the end of the world for me. It doesn't mean I spend days sitting on the sofa eating chocolate, crisps, can after can of beer, pizza, etc., far from it; in fact, I am prone to not eating if I'm busy rather than eating complete rubbish like that. Which also isn't good for me. If I was the person on the sofa with the TV on eating what I just described above every night, then seriously, it would be time to make some changes. Getting out of the habit would be high on my list of priorities instead of eating all that shit and lying for days on the sofa not producing any good. We need to be properly fueled in body and mind to recognise what we want in life and to stand up for it and go get it.

I am not a nutritionist, doctor, pharmacist, dietitian, personal trainer or anything like that. I do not have a piece of paper that says I am qualified to tell anyone what to do, etc. But, what I do have is a lot of experience in eating well, being advised on my diet, and being extremely aware of what foods do to me and for me as I train and prepare for surfing huge waves so that I am at a permanent high level of fitness and always motivated despite not knowing exactly when I may be able to go on a big wave mission due to the unpredictability of the weather in this part of the Atlantic.

I know a lot of people have a bad diet at times through inability to cook. I am not a good cook, and to be honest, I hate cooking. However, I think these basic things fuel my body and the mind in the most natural way, and if they are included and form the largest part of my diet, then there is less chance or room to put something which maybe isn't so good into my body.

This is how I fuel myself; everyone requires a different diet for various reasons, so I cannot give anyone advice on what to take in. I am merely showing what I use to fuel myself in the knowledge that it works for me. If you are reading this and want to seek nutritional advice, then I suggest you speak to a suitably qualified professional just as I did. They will cater for your lifestyle, your abilities, your goals, etc. In this instance, I recommend Richard Robinson, World Natural Middleweight Bodybuilding Champion. This man is expert in diet and safely manipulating training and food intake for all sorts of reasons and goals.

The foods I use in various combinations at various stages of the year and depending upon what I'm working on achieving are as follows ...

Breakfasts

Eggs (various combinations of whites and yolks depending on goal)

Porridge (made with milk)

Shake (consisting of various combinations of protein powder, banana, oats, milk, berries, peanut butter, spirulina, seeds, creatine)

Lunches / dinners

Fish, chicken, steak (the odd time)

Leaves, tomatoes, broccoli, carrots, nuts, seeds, beans

Potato, rice, pasta, brown bread

Olive oil, balsamic vinegar, whole grain mustard

Fruit juice, milk, water

Fruit

I am not a good cook to be honest, and I stick to mainly whole foods in my diet, and I also make curries, pastas, and chili in large batches to re-heat throughout the week.

I also eat takeaways when I'm being a bad boy. I find I want to eat more rubbish when I haven't been eating properly.

Anyway, this is not supposed to be a painstaking look at diet in a big way and is by no means exhaustive or precise or meant to be copied. I'm just showing the basic ingredients to my diet that I believe allow me personally to stay alert, energized, capable, and ready always to do whatever I want or need to. I firmly believe diet contributes massively to attitude and mood and, therefore, our ability to handle things in life that get in our way. Some fears and anxieties require a lot of effort to overcome, and by fueling the body and mind correctly for our own personal individual circumstances, I believe we give ourselves a massive advantage in avoiding taking the perceived easy option, a different route or path, and instead working on dealing with whatever is in our way and progressing through to new opportunities, new experiences, and a fulfilled life of achievement and satisfaction.

24

HOW MUCH DO YOU WANT IT?

Seriously, how much do you want the thing on the other side of the fear? This thing that's stopping you getting what you want – is it greater than your desire to have whatever it is you are trying to accomplish? Sometimes, it's as simple as that. Maybe you need to evaluate your desire for what you think your goal is. It may be that you don't want it enough to then want to deal with the fear you are experiencing to get it. If that's the case, then I personally would turn away. There's no shame in that; there's plenty of other things and experiences in life I probably want more in some cases so could focus my energy on those. If I don't want something, then why would I pursue the thing? Peer pressure or anything else should never be a deciding factor in anyone's desire to go after something, especially if it scares them. I've seen a lot of people think they want to be big wave surfers, they think they are Billy Big Balls because they surf the odd bigger day at the local beach and next they are banging on about surfing Mullaghmore Head or something like that! They get themselves all psyched up; they believe their own hype without any real understanding of the difference between surfing the local beach at any size compared to the hell they will experience on a proper huge day at Mullaghmore if they f£$k up! If they even ever get themselves the right gear; it's usually the norm that when they turn up the sound, the energy, the environment is a total shock to the system, and they gradually disappear. Very few people have the desire or ability to push through when they are faced with fear on that level. Some will go away, rethink, and come back better prepared, 99% won't. Both are totally acceptable outcomes if it's what that person wants or doesn't want, and that is why fear is there. It gives us time and lets us decide what we really want and if we want to face that fear to get it.

I have personally seen a couple of people out at spots including Mullaghmore Head who quite honestly should not be out there. They have not evaluated the risk and their ability, and they are way out of their depth. It puts the fear of God into them as they are underprepared in various ways, and the fear drives them away never to pursue big waves again. It's such a shame because I know the benefits facing anxieties and fear can have if time is taken to sharpen the blade before tackling them head on. A step back, re-think, re-evaluate and prepare before heading into it head-on would probably work for a lot of people, but in every walk of life, including big wave surfing, people misjudge situations and quickly find themselves out of their depth. They are swamped by fear and panic, and then understandably run a mile never to return to that thing they dreamt about, built up to in their heads. It's such a shame when that happens. It's so important to take a step back when scared if time allows it – evaluate, observe, learn, prepare and then if it's something we really want once the risks, the consequences of doing or not doing have all been weighed up, either move forward towards the fear or move forwards in another direction that is more suitable. It's very important to remember that just because someone may decide something they once thought was for them isn't, that that is not seen as failure; if anything, it's a win. Letting go of something that isn't for us takes huge balls and commitment and commands as much respect as facing fears. Sometimes the fear of failure is greater than the fear of pushing through to a goal. Failure is only failure if we stop dead in our tracks. If we keep moving, we never fail, we just change our direction through life and continue to move forwards. Fears that cause us to stop and go another way because we decide we don't want the thing we once thought we did do not mean life is over, they do not mean we have failed, it's over, the end. It simply means by deciding we don't want that thing we thought that we did, we open ourselves to opportunity for something else. The terrible thing is when fear stands in the way and stops us getting the thing we really want. That's when we must dig deep.

In 2003, I went on my first trip to Northern California to surf a famous big wave surf spot called Mavericks. The waves didn't get big enough for the spot to break for about three weeks, and in that time, I was able to train at other spots in preparation for surfing Mavericks, if I was lucky enough to get the opportunity. I had travelled there with six big wave boards and bought another one out there. I had lots of experience in big waves at home, and I had the right equipment for the trip. I had been training specifically for this trip for six months! I put myself through rigorous training and diet to be as prepared as I could be. I studied every video and picture of the spot and the guys surfing there. In the 4th week of my trip, I got lucky, and Mavericks broke several times. On the first day, I was very scared and anxious. I hadn't slept properly, and it was a surreal feeling being in the place I had dreamt of surfing since I was 13! I was with all the guys I looked up to and was being guided by them at their spot. When we first paddled out, I took the approach of watching it from the safety of the deep-water channel. I watched other guys going on huge waves. It was amazing. I even got caught by a huge set that I had to swim through, and I was OK. I spent eight hours out there that day, and virtually the entire daylight was spent in the water trying to catch a wave. I was the last one to leave the water when it was almost dark with my mate shouting at me telling me it was time to go. I pussied out! The day I dreamt of all my life to that point – it was right there. I was prepared, and yet, I couldn't handle it. I was intimidated. I was too scared to commit. All the horror stories of other guys getting smashed, etc. were in my head, and I couldn't focus on doing what I wanted to do. I was angry at myself and reluctantly paddled back ashore in the dusk feeling like a complete and utter loser! I couldn't believe I did that. I went away and had a serious talk with myself! I was fortunate to get several more opportunities that week to pull myself together and get the job done! I spent several sessions out there catching waves, going through wipeouts and all the rest. I did what I went there to do, and I was extremely proud of myself for various things in the end. I hit a wall of fear the first day, and despite smashing it with all that I had and banging my head on said wall, I couldn't break through. I went away, and I got smart; I spent a couple of days calling myself names and reaffirming my ability to myself, and I returned and pulled it off. That dream for me began at the age of 13 when I first saw pictures and videos of Mavericks, and at the age of 22, I went there. I almost f£$ked it up completely because I was scared, and I froze up, but in the end, I gave myself a shake and got it done. That gave me real direction in life; it gave me huge confidence in myself and gave me detailed knowledge of how I might react in the future, and ultimately, how to deal with it!

25

What's Best?

For me, if there is something that really matters, something that is necessary, something that I must do, I want, I need, fear and anxiety stand absolutely no chance most of the time. I keep going, it's the only way. If I stop too long, the conditions, the elements they become overwhelming, they sink the boat so to speak.

Education and Knowledge. Learning as much as possible about the thing that the anxiety is coming from. Learning all there is to know with the goal of eliminating as many unknown quantities as possible and moving forward with the knowledge that I'm ready for whatever comes my way and I will get through. Sometimes it's impossible to rule out all the unknown quantities, but even the slightest bit more knowledge than before shines a little more light into the dark and it becomes easier to see more clearly.

The best action I find to work against fear is *Anger*. Anger focuses me, I'm good at being angry with myself or the situation! But seriously, it is something which just seems to happen on the very brink of something happening. It is a rare occasion for me to use this but on the rare occasion that I am fearful in the heat of the moment I will growl it out and suddenly, the mind switches from being a victim of fear to be a warrior, standing tall and fighting through it to overcome, not succumb! It allows me over the ledge so to speak and helps me achieve the thing I want to do.

I do not know the circumstances, the experiences or the life of anyone reading my experiences in this book. I wish I was able to advise people with a generic one size fits all type of thing that would easily help people but unfortunately that's not what fear and anxiety allow. I really hope that by reading my experiences here that people can benefit in some way in their battles with their own anxiety and fear in finding their own way to handle it. I know that everyone has different challenges. Some more severe, some less severe than others but there is always a way. The mind is vaster than the ocean itself. That vastness can lead to all sorts of problems, but it can also lead to all sorts of solutions. There are lots of challenging elements but there are also lots of beneficial elements. The most important thing I have found is that no matter what it is, if its something that is important then never give up, do whatever it takes to break through. For me, there have been times I have pulled back or not committed and its left me wondering. There is nothing better than being able to look back knowing that I committed to whatever it was and succeeded in something with or without fear.

One More thing....

If you manage to face your fears or anxiety and can explain how, then do what you can to help the next person.

About the author

Al Mennie is a Big Wave Surfer, Paddleboarder, Ocean Explorer, Author, Adventurer and 3rd degree black belt. He lives life on the edge on the rugged north coast of Ireland with his fiancée, designer Sara O'Neill, and their retriever, Blyton.

Al Mennie is the epitome of an athlete pushing the boundaries both physically and mentally. Al was one of the originals, the man who first began launching boats and jet-skis in Ireland in pursuit of giant waves and the first person to push the barriers of what is possible in our ocean.

Al has pioneered and surfed big wave spots in Ireland and globally. He thrives in wild conditions off his native shoreline.

Since 2003 Al has searched, discovered, located and pioneered several big wave spots. He rode the record-breaking storm on December 1st, 2007 at Mullaghmore Head when the biggest swell ever recorded in the Atlantic Ocean smashed into Ireland. Al worked with American surfer Garrett McNamara in Nazare Portugal over a three-year period in the early days of tackling huge waves off the Portuguese coast. Al was one of four men in the water the day the biggest waves ever ridden swung into Nazaré in Portugal.

In every sense of the word he is a waterman. Other than pushing the limits of big-wave surfing he has also paddled a surfboard from Ireland to Scotland, against the tide, and has a reputation as having one of the most grueling and effective training regimes in the world; his activities range from rock running on the ocean floor to being held underwater by his trainer after sprinting up his local sand dunes. At 6'5" and with a large beard (mountain man not hipster) he is a triple black belt and an imposing but gentle figure. Al has also written a memoir, Surfing

Mennie Waves, available at bookstores across Ireland and the UK. Always articulate, he enjoys a media profile that transcends surfing.

Overcome or Succumb

Overcome or Succumb

243

Image Credits

Cover Image by Wilson Ribeiro

Page 241 – Middle row LHS image by Sara O'Neill

Page 243 – Middle row image by Sara O'Neill

Bottom row – Middle jet ski image by Rich Murphy

Page 244 – Second Row – RHS Image by Leigh Hawthorne

Bottom image Al Dwarfed image by Andrew Hill Troggs Surf Shop

Page 245 – Top Nazare image by Wilson Ribeiro

Bottom left image by Andrew Hill Troggs Surf Shop

All other Images by Al Mennie

Images Featuring – Al Mennie, Leigh Hawthorne, Tim Howell, Charles McQuillan, Hanno Windisch

@wrphotos_wr

charlesmcquillan.com

richmurphyphotography.com

snuggwetsuits.co.uk

troggs.com

almennie.com

Al Mennie

Overcome or Succumb